LIVING PEACE

Essential Teachings for
Enlightenment in the 21st Century

By

Alaric Hutchinson

EARTH SPIRIT PUBLISHING

LIVING PEACE: Essential Teachings for Enlightenment in the 21st Century
Copyright © 2014, 2018 by Alaric K. Hutchinson. Earth Spirit Publishing, LLC.

The Zen Cowboy
P.O. Box 991
Bayfield, CO 81122
www.ZenCowboy.org

First Edition: July 2014
Second Edition: December 2018

ISBN: 978-0-9904058-7-0

Dedication

I dedicate this book to the world. May these teachings serve as a touchstone that will allow all of humanity to learn and embody the ways of peace. And one day, when we reach the stars, may these teachings continue to grow and thrive, spreading peace throughout the Universe.

Table of Contents

An Introduction to the Second Edition

Reviewing and revising *Living Peace* four years after its initial publication has been quite refreshing. Although I live and teach this material every day, each time I read through the entire book, I am always surprised. Every return to *Living Peace* reminds me how enlightening the teachings truly are. Nonetheless, in this edition, each chapter has received a makeover — in some chapters, the changes were minor, while others required a major rewrite. That said, each tenet's essence remains the same, as their wisdoms are Universal. Every update was done to help further define the teachings and explain the concepts more effectively, since my teaching and communication skills have increased beyond the first publication.

The biggest change of note concerns the layout of this book. Each tenet now has the corresponding practice included in its chapter, and the nine tenets have been broken down into three parts with additional coaching starting off each section, such as Explaining Ego at the start of Part One. These changes, along with content that's been removed from the original — such as the Notes & Quotes section — allow for a more organized study and an easier read.

An additional advantage of time passing is that I have been able to see firsthand how these teachings have impacted and changed lives. Inner peace truly is the by-product of living and breathing these teachings. Change will certainly come — if you allow it and are consistent with your practice. My hope, dear reader, is that you take these teachings to heart and find great benefit in applying the practices to your life.

Alaric Hutchinson

The Living Peace Code

P.E.A.C.E.
People Embracing **A** Conscious Evolution

I **AM** the Master of my Life:
I Master my Thoughts.
I Master my Impulses.
I Master my Emotions.

I see **THROUGH** Illusion:
There is no Ignorance.
There is no Chaos.
There is no Duality.

I Forever **SEEK** and Cultivate:
Understanding,
Harmony, and
Transcendence.

Everything is Impermanent. Change is the only Constant.

I RELEASE my Attachments to the Mundane World.
I RELEASE my Attachments to What I Know.
I RELEASE my Attachments to Who I Am.
I RELINQUISH… **My SELF**…

I **AM**
P.E.A.C.E.
People Embodying **A** Conscious Evolution

The Living Peace Code Explained

Living Peace can be seen through a spiritual lens, or a purely philosophical lens; however, having an open mind towards the underlying spiritual tones of this book will certainly assist in further expanding your awareness as you make your way through the teachings. Since its first publication, I have taught these tenets to people of nearly every religion (and those of non-faith) alongside a wide range of political affiliations. Peace is a universal and humanitarian desire—a truly unifying force on our planet, regardless of our differing backgrounds. Yet, even with this awareness, peace is still something that is a struggle to create and maintain in our world. Many answers to this dilemma are found within this book, giving you the means to create peace on both micro and macro levels throughout the rest of your life.

≫ ≫ ≫ ≪ ≪ ≪

The Living Peace Code and its nine tenets came to me within minutes after I sat down one evening with the intention to meditate on what my life message was—to write, to teach, and to live. I was taken aback by how quickly the code appeared within my mind's eye. I wasted no time expanding upon each of the tenets over the course of the year that followed. I began teaching them to my students, sharing them during Sunday services, and eventually the wisdom took full form in the creation of this book.

At the time of the creation of *Living Peace*, my life was a bit hectic and remained so for a few more years. It's curious how one can receive so much knowledge and yet not fully live it! Peace ultimately comes down to choice and enough awareness to step out of our own way (ego). As I write these words now, nearing completion of this revised edition, I can attest that my life — my marriage, business, community, family, and overall wellbeing — has forever been changed for the better because of these teachings.

As you read through this book, I'll be sharing with you some personal stories that showcase just how far I have come in a very short time, and it's all thanks to this lifestyle of literally *Living Peace*.

Although the nine tenets flow seamlessly together, I've broken them down into three separate segments known as Masteries, Illusions, & Attachments. Especially during my coaching and student trainings, I have found that this way of absorbing the information is incredibly helpful. So, as you venture onward into the depths of this book, you will see Parts One, Two, and Three creating distinct pauses between the three tenet segments. At the beginning of each part, you'll also notice an introductory concept that adds further depth and imparts important information for the upcoming tenets.

For your first perusal through this book, I recommend that you read straight through rather than jumping around or pausing too long between each chapter or part. Do not worry if you don't fully comprehend a tenet; if you keep reading, more and more pieces of the puzzle will come together to create the full, rich portrait this book aims to provide you with — one that depicts the enlightened lifestyle of *Living Peace*. After your first read-through, you are then invited to start over. The second time, I encourage you to take your approach more slowly, methodically applying each new practice to your life as you go along. Once both read-throughs are complete, the jumping around can commence for easy reference and enjoyability!

I share the above recommendations because, since the first publication of *Living Peace*, I've encountered several people who didn't want to progress with the reading until they had fully applied the wisdom of each chapter. Although this way of reading an action-oriented, philosophical book is sometimes very useful, for the purpose of *Living Peace,* it's much more efficient to first read the entirety of the book because the Living Peace Code is constructed in a circle, not a ladder. As you will soon see, the tenets weave in and out of each other, creating a living, breathing tapestry of an enlightened lifestyle anyone can use, one that applies to every area of a person's life.

≫ ≫ ≫ ≪ ≪ ≪

Before we begin our journey into the nine tenets, I find it beneficial for students and readers to first be introduced to the 5 Layers of Consciousness. These layers are a fascinating revelation of how consciousness impacts our lives; thus, having a basic understanding of each layer greatly assists in learning the *Living Peace* tenets and practices.

Note: the 5 Layers of Consciousness were revealed to me during a meditation shortly after the Living Peace Code's creation.

The 5 Layers of Consciousness

The Five Layers of Consciousness are "onion peel" realities that we exist in and pass through each and every day. Many people assume that there is only one reality, the reality they see through their own eyes. This, dear reader, is one of the greatest illusions, and you'll soon emerge from its haze (or "awaken") as you continue reading.

As you venture forward into understanding the 5 Layers of Consciousness, imagine that each layer is a circle — the Mundane in the middle has the smallest circumference, and the Cosmic outer ring encircling the rest has the greatest circumference.

Found within these layers are the answers to why there is such great spiritual, religious, cultural and political diversity on our planet. Billions of people experience our world through different layers of consciousness. Who is right? Who is wrong? Both and neither. They are just living out varying degrees of the same collective world.

Let's dive in now and see what stories each layer holds and learn why it's important to understand each before we begin our lessons on the Living Peace Code.

The Mundane Consciousness

The Mundane Consciousness is the reality that we perceive with our first five senses instead of fully activating our sixth sense, which is *mind*. Existing at this level of consciousness means seeing and accepting the world at face value. This surface consciousness works well for many people, since it is the easiest to comprehend. They simply live the same lifestyle that they were brought up in without really questioning it. This way of thinking embraces the stereotypical concepts that men are raised to be good workers, soldiers, and husbands, and women are raised to be good homemakers, mothers, and wives.

In this layer of consciousness, attachment, ego, and duality are simply part of everyday life. There is right and wrong, there is good and bad, and — in the case of those who follow religious dogma — there is also holiness and sinfulness. In truth, many people live full and happy lives within this consciousness, so long as they play by the rules and don't attempt to step outside social norms.

But more often, people in the Mundane Consciousness suffer the most due their attachments, their egos, and their dualistic beliefs. When we do not realize there is more to life than meets the eye, we cling like barnacles to what we already possess and what we have come to believe as true about the world, even if what we have or what we believe in is causing ourselves or others pain. Instead of focusing on self-growth and allowing change, we focus on controlling the people and situations in our lives, often out of fear of change.

It's difficult to "awaken" people from the Mundane Consciousness; however, their awakening will naturally occur in time. Everyone is on their own path, and it is not for us to judge others or try to force them to grow. Some people are born awake and open to the expanded layers of consciousness and other people progress into higher levels through inspiration, while some individuals only find the next layer by first hitting rock bottom and bouncing back up.

A common question is, "Why do major tragedies continue to occur on our planet?" The answer is that when individuals are faced with the pain and contrast found within a tragedy, they're presented with the choice: to stay in the Mundane mindset or rise to the occasion with compassion and cooperation. What is beautiful about this is that it is inherent in our DNA to adapt to situations and to help one another. Thus, Mundane Consciousness evolves into Collective Consciousness.

Note: As global consciousness continues to rise, the masses will also rise out of functioning predominately from ego and duality. The result? Less human-born tragedies will occur. This is the conjoined relationship Consciousness shares with Growth: people behave in more harmful ways in the first two layers of consciousness, yet it is the pain this harm causes that actually awakens them. Truly fascinating!

The Collective Consciousness

The Collective Consciousness is the layer in which people begin to think beyond themselves and empathize with the happenings of the world. It is within the Mundane and Collective layers that the majority of this planet's people reside.

In the Collective Consciousness, people acknowledge the mundane and strive to transcend their attachments to materialism, superficiality, and the "drama of it all" — yet they still struggle with ego and duality. Self-righteousness is also a common obstacle in this layer. Here, most religious and political movements aimed at helping the world can be found; but many involved "miss the mark" which prevents unity and peace because they are still perpetuating entitlement and dualistic beliefs. As long as there is a group of people who believe that they are right, and all others are wrong, we will have human-inflicted pain and separation on this earth.

Another characteristic present in the Collective Consciousness is the "hive-mind" mentality. Our egos become inflated when we attach ourselves to a group of like-minded individuals. We feel powerful. We feel supported. And we feel secure. Sometimes, we may even feel loved; however, this form of love is conditional, dependent upon cooperation within the group. Often, when one aspect of the hive-mind's purpose, ideal, or community is questioned, the majority takes offence, even if the dissenting mindset does not affect them as individuals. In belonging to a group, loss of individuality occurs and is replaced by the collective consciousness.

A fascinating aspect of the hive-mindset occurs when members throw away reason and rational thinking for the sake of being part of the group. Historically, this may have served its purpose in creating modern society by bringing people together to achieve common goals for survival. Now our call to action is to transcend this mentality and never compromise our integrity, kindness and logic for the sake of blindly following a group's (or even a single person's) ideals.

How many of us today consider ourselves members of a certain religious or political group, yet we have little actual knowledge of how it functions and what tenets it embraces? Too often, a heedless lack of research and/or questioning results in blindly counting ourselves among the ranks of certain groups. We make life-altering decisions for ourselves and others concerning issues we know very little about. We can see this happening in the way we raise our children, vote, go to war, discriminate against others, place our trust in established institutions, make our purchases, and collectively live our lives.

The reason the hive-mind mentality exists is because it is easier to be a follower than it is to be the leaders of our own lives. It's all too convenient to let other people tell us how to live, how to vote, and what to believe in rather than spend great chunks of time and energy educating ourselves enough to reach our own conclusions. A huge benefit of being a follower is not having to do the work. This provides us with more time to do what we enjoy, even if the downside means we are consistently uninformed.

Eventually, when things go wrong, instead of taking personal responsibility for our chosen lack of awareness, we blame the people or institutions we have put our blind trust in.

The hive-mind mentality is extremely volatile and easily turns into mob mentality.

The mob mentality can occur when the hive-mind mentality implodes. When our everyday reality is unexpectedly taken from us, fear occurs, identity is lost, and we can go into a daze that limits rational thinking. That's when we react rather than respond. And when there's a group of people all experiencing this dazed distress at the same time, mobs capable of wreaking great social havoc form.

However, if each person had inner peace, was capable of critical thinking and reasoning, took responsibility for their lives and actions without placing blame, something very different would occur. No matter what happened on the planet, no matter how extensive the tragedies — or how numerous — each and every person would pause before reacting and respond with peace and intelligence, rather than perpetuate chaos and fear. Humanity would thrive and unite, rather than splinter once again into discriminating groups who find it necessary to fight.

This is why it is so important for each of us to be independent thinkers and join groups and communities because they resonate within our hearts and promote our creative individuality rather than suppress our authentic selves by using fear as a means to coerce us to conform.

We begin to move to Transcendent Consciousness when we realize that the security promised by others in the Collective Consciousness is an illusion.

Often, this realization is reached when we hit rock bottom in our lives or become "black sheep" in our community. Because the hive mind of politics and religions often adheres to specific rules and ideals, the moment we disagree or no longer can comply with what is expected, we become social outcasts. Although things are changing in our modern era, examples of this are the huge taboo it sometimes still is to marry someone from a different religion or divorcing. People who were once kind to us now judge us, and the gold that gilded our once-strong belief system and community begins to flake off.

An example that hits close to home is watching when gay friends are immediately disowned by their families and excommunicated from their religious communities when they come "out of the closet".

In the Collective Consciousness, people often sacrifice the freedom of authenticity for the promise of security. But when individuals begin to place more value on being authentic than on conditional security, they eventually find themselves among those who live in Transcendent Consciousness. Ironically, unconditional security is found right alongside pure authenticity within that layer.

I consider this the evolution from homo-sapiens (wise-men) to homo-luminous. Our spirits and consciousness evolve rather than our physical bodies. As previously mentioned, the hive-mind may once have served the necessary purpose of survival, but we are now entering into a new era in which individual responsibility and co-creation are of greater value to the progression of our planet.

The Transcendent Consciousness

Transcendent Consciousness pertains to the stage of growing self-awareness. It is often uncomfortable. In the Mundane or Collective Consciousness, it is easy to cast blame and judgment via anger or self-righteousness; however, in the layer of Transcendent Consciousness, we begin to realize that all happiness or suffering stems from our own attitudes, perspectives, and the choices we've made in our lives. With this self-accounting, there's no longer room for blame. Nor can we pass responsibility for our dissatisfaction with our lives on to anyone else — it's all us: past, present, and future. This so-called awakening (transcending the ego) can be bittersweet since we're no longer able to live in ignorant bliss.

A compact definition of Transcendent Consciousness is: an individual grows into and eventually has consistent awareness that they are not their thoughts, feelings, or emotions. They begin to notice the difference between their egoic impulses and beliefs, and those of their higher, unbiased self (residing in the part of our minds that can observe the ego as if from a bird's eye view). This is when the concept of nonduality begins to make sense and begins to be applied, which is something we will explore in depth later in this book.

Over the years several students have shared with me the difficulty of achieving this layer of consciousness. On one hand, they think it's beautiful to recognize just how much power of choice they have over their minds, bodies and overall quality of life. On the other, they feel it can also be daunting and overwhelming. Additionally, they learn how all of their thoughts, words, and actions influence the combined consciousness and vibration of the world due to the universal law of cause and effect. This awareness can lead to pain or feelings of guilt over their pasts — previously, they may have been blind to how their actions influenced others; now they realize just how much weight every word and action carries. Thus, for some, this is the "make or break" stage in this layer of consciousness on their journey towards inner peace.

They may choose to go back to living in the Collective Consciousness simply because they are not ready to release the duality of right and wrong, good and bad, etc. They may still cling to the stories of their pain, which perpetuates their suffering, all the while receiving a twisted form of validation through the pity they receive as victims. Hard words to hear. No one likes viewing themselves as a victim since it puts them in a place of powerlessness, and yet that's what they make themselves into when they become trapped by negative emotions and thought patterns.

Transcendent Consciousness is also where spiritually aware individuals sometimes become blinded by their egos. We often do so much "self" work that we begin to feel like we "know" better than others. It is imperative that we stay out of this mindset. Attaching ourselves to all the hard work, studying, and healing we have done, as well as over-relating to our accomplishments, can cause us to slip back into our egoic selves, often at the expense of further learning. If we are judgmental in any way — of others or ourselves — it signals that we have more work to do with our egos in this layer. Again, those in the Collective Consciousness are unaware of their egos (or forget), while those in Transcendent Consciousness are fully aware of ego and practice daily to transcend it.

As I write about ego and use layers as a means of teaching, let me be very clear that this discussion in no way, shape, or form is meant to become a vehicle by which to judge others or to compare one's self to anyone else. "I'm here and you're there" is a judgment. In truth, none of us is ever capable of fully discerning how far another person is along their path. Even contemplating where other people are at in relation to where we are is ego* stimulation, which can only create further separation. The purpose of these layers is only to help us as individuals understand where *we* are at in the moment and where *we* can go to from here, especially since we may shift in and out of these layers of consciousness on a daily, hourly, or even momentary, basis.

*Note: *Ego will be fully defined in Explaining the Ego chapter. For now, a helpful tip to understanding ego is that it's the part of our mind that pushes, pulls, and holds onto things. Often accompanied by negative emotion — our egoic mind encourages us to push away and resist what we don't like, hold tight onto what we fear losing, and chase after our desires. These three aspects of ego all lead to further separation due to the judgments and negative emotions that arise from resisting life's natural impermanence (constant change).*

The Galactic Consciousness

In evolving through the stages of Transcendent Consciousness, eventually all forms of human attachment are called to the forefront of our minds. A mixture of sadness and joyfulness takes up residence as we start to see all life through the eyes of impermanence, which renders all forms of attachment moot. Nothing lasts, and so each experience is seen as delicious and beautiful in the raw moment — yet sadness is also present, especially regarding loved ones. Because life is fleeting, we are aware our moments with them will soon pass, not to be relived. And so, when the death experience eventually comes to us all, we embrace it without fear, just as each droplet of water evaporates only to rain down upon the Earth again for another "life" cycle.

We enter into the Galactic Consciousness when we are no longer in denial of our own impermanence, nor are we afraid of it. We're able to observe life consistently through the lens of our higher selves, where no dualistic judgments or egoic resistance is present. There is a natural acceptance that pervades all thought — which is joyfully sad. Please take note not to confuse this version of sadness with the sadness found in the lower layers of consciousness. This joyful sadness is not negative or depressing in the slightest; rather, it is neutral and the natural byproduct of fully seeing life in its wholeness, which is tear-jerkingly beautiful and yet impermanent. At the heart of this joyful sadness lies gratitude.

In the Galactic Consciousness, we maintain our inner peace, no matter what the external conditions or situations may be. Egoistic judgment does not exist in the Galactic Consciousness, whereas in the Transcendent Consciousness a person may make a judgment, catch it before it is spoken, and turn the judgement around into a positive thought. In Galactic

Consciousness, there is no need for this type of "second thought" since the first thought is already in complete alignment with peaceful acceptance. Additionally, we cease to analyze whether or not we are in a certain layer of consciousness, and without effort, we begin to live consistently in the present moment. Again, peace pervades.

On the cusp of the Galactic Consciousness, just before entering into the Cosmic Consciousness, we find our saints, bodhisattvas, and ascended masters. These are individuals who have presumably achieved enlightenment and have chosen to remain as guides for us. Some believe they reincarnate as souls with advanced awareness, to help all of humanity cross over to the Cosmic. Others believe these saints and masters continue to be present in nonphysical form, gently guiding us along the path towards spiritual awakening. Whatever your unique, personal belief may be on the matter of afterlife is not relevant right now. What is important for the sake of this teaching, is that all of us may gain inspiration from those who came before us and achieved states of inner peace, like Buddha, who proved that we are all capable of *Living Peace.*

One magical night at my parents' home, they, my husband, and I witnessed the first snowfall since our move to Colorado. We were high up in the mountains when the flakes began to float down, all happy, warm, and cozy inside—observing their beauty through the large windows. My mom reached for my hand with a smile and said, "Let us remember this moment forever." She looked so beautiful and peaceful as she gazed out into the sky, and it was as if I was glimpsing into her past when she was a little girl in West Virginia watching the snow fall with her mother. That loving moment was forever embedded into my heart. I later shared my glimpse with my husband, expressing that it had made me feel joy

and sadness all at the same time.

During that beautiful moment with my mom, it seemed as if time had stopped to intermingle past, present, and future. I had stepped outside my body to become simply an observer witnessing the miracle of life. The sadness was not the usual sadness of grief or upset, but rather a beautiful sadness honoring that everything we as humans experience, including our very lives, is temporary— born to fade and pass away. Nothing lasts. We cannot hold a snowflake long before it melts, nor can we hold onto moments long before they become memories that fade. This is what it means to be alive, and that night I felt the joyful sadness that came with touching and accepting the wisdom of the Galactic Consciousness.

The Cosmic Consciousness

Last but not least, is the Cosmic Consciousness, which is what we may individually call Spirit, the Universe, God, etc. The analogy I teach is that Cosmic Consciousness can be seen as a Cosmic Ocean. We are all part of it, yet we are mere droplets that make up its infinite waters. We simply do not have the cognitive ability in our human, physical form to comprehend its vastness. This limitation of understanding is neither good nor bad; it just is.

When each of us purifies our soul, or droplet of water, the entire ocean becomes purer — as does the Universe. It, too, raises vibration and expands "consciousness". Thus, through our own growth and expansion, the Universe expands and grows with us.

How can the droplet understand the vastness of the ocean? By looking within. For the droplet and ocean are made of the same cosmic substance. As above, so below. As within, so without. When we can understand the depths of our own soul, we then begin to more clearly understand the vastness of the Universe.

Although my ego wishes to give more information here, any attempt to do so would be simply a guess. How can anyone explain the nature of God or the Universe? Religions attempt to understand God, and scientists attempt to understand the Universe. I like to think the Truth exists somewhere in the middle of their postulations.

Perpetual Expansion through Faith

As a disclaimer, faith is not a word I often use, however, it is extremely fitting for this section. Faith, or trust, is what allows us to traverse the layers of consciousness, since we are only ever able to step backwards into them. Imagine starting in the middle, in the Mundane, and walking backwards until you reach the Cosmic. The reason we walk "backwards" in this analogy is because our sight is limited to our degree of awareness—thus when we are in the Transcendent Consciousness, we can look in front of us to recognize the Mundane and Collective for what they are, but we have yet to see the Galactic or Cosmic. That leap of faith must be taken before we will have any hope of understanding.

It's important to note that no person is ever wrong in the way they experience their reality. Because humans live in, and traverse, different layers, conflicting messages come through various channels within those layers. For example, a reverend who resides in the Collective Consciousness and preaches holy scripture will have a different perspective on the message than a reverend residing in the Galactic Consciousness preaching the same scripture. The reverend who resides in the Galactic would most likely be unsuccessful in changing the perspective of the reverend residing in the Collective, and vice versa. Multiple versions of the same truth exist at the same time and just vary in degree.

In order to reach Cosmic Consciousness, we must continue to expand our horizons—which often means stepping outside our comfort zones. And often, what makes us most uncomfortable offers us our greatest opportunities for growth. In many situations, it takes a leap of faith—bravely walking into the unknown then taking a step backwards in order to see the "big picture". We take steps back not knowing where our feet will land, yet with each backward stride, we see reality more clearly. Step by step, more information is revealed to us as we come closer to Cosmic Consciousness.

A useful analogy for relating to 5 Layers of Consciousness is imagining a house. When we are in the Mundane, we are inside our house. All we can see is our home, our belongings, and the people within. We are very much attached to everything and everyone inside our house and pay little attention to anything or anyone outside.

In the Collective, we now have a bird's eye view above our house. We are a bit less attached to our home, yet we can still see it from above. Now we are also able to see our neighborhood and a few other locations off in the distance. For example, we may be able to see our church and its members, our town and place of work, and our children's school. We live a more open life in the Collective, yet we still find ourselves very much attached to the life we have created. It simply holds more people and things.

The Transcendent is where things literally become a bit ungrounded. What this means is that we are now so high up in elevation that we mostly see clouds. We can only briefly glimpse anything below us, and everything appears ant-sized. This is a bit scary because we have no solid ground to stand upon nor anything familiar to cling to and make us feel safe and secure. In this layer, we begin to realize that any attachments we have are moot, because we cannot hold onto them, anyway. Eventually, we learn to accept our groundless situation and find peace within it.

In the Galactic, we are now above the Earth, peering down as if from a satellite. We are much removed from our old, personalized, human lives, our previous individual bubbles of awareness, so we now see everything on a global scale and care more for humanity and the planet as a whole.

In the Cosmic, we finally reach far out into space, our awareness spanning the Universe and our being focused primarily upon the vibrations of love and peace rather than on the impermanent tangibles of human existence. There is no longer the least sense of ego, attachment, or duality. To the Universe, a human life is but a blink of an eye, yet with each blink miracles occur and beauty is ours to behold.

Concluding Thoughts

I have only given a brief overview of the layers here. As you read through this book the layers are excellent reference points to use when checking in with where you are at along your journey. Keep in mind that we often phase in and out of multiple layers throughout any given day depending on our vibration and perceptions.

Part One:

The Three Masteries

The Ego Explained

Simply put, ego is the aspect of mind that feels separate from the world and likes to reinforce said separation. It may have served a very necessary part in our human evolution up to this point—especially regarding our fight or flight response—yet now, since taming this once primal world, we no longer need to act on our animalistic survival impulses that cause us to physically or psychologically "go to war" with anyone or anything that threatens us. In fact, it is our ego that keeps the very nature of war alive on our planet. As humanity increasingly awakens to the awareness of ego and ceases to let it guide their thoughts, words, and actions, we will begin to see increasing peace throughout the world, and the way we treat our planet will be to replenish rather than destroy it.

An easy way I explain ego to my students is through the "Push, Pull, Hold Tight" example. Before we jump into the first three tenets of the Living Peace Code, a solid understanding of how our ego exists and operates within us is necessary. Please feel free to return to this chapter for clarity as you read through the tenets, as you will surely begin to see the correlation between the ego and the pain-inflicting role it plays in many aspects of our human lives.

Push, Pull, Hold Tight:

When we push against anything in life, this is the part of our ego that is filled with dislikes acting out. Anything that causes us discomfort or pain, we resist and attempt to push it away or push it down. Pushing often manifests as impatience, frustration, and anger—key phrase being "resisting life".

Pulling, or grasping, is the part of our ego that is filled

with likes. Anything we feel will bring us pleasure, satisfaction, or happiness we may find ourselves grasping for, chasing after, and pulling towards us. Pulling can manifest as flightiness, neurotic euphoria, or extreme highs followed by extreme lows — often accompanied by low self-worth, defeatism, and even depression. Key phrase for pulling is "chasing life".

Holding tight comes from the part of our ego that is insecure, doubtful, and afraid. Whatever comforts give us the sense of security or love that we currently have (even when subpar) become the things we hold tight to and fear parting with since "something is better than nothing". This often takes the form of not wanting to let go of abusive relationships, toxic work environments, and addictions — even when they are destroying our lives. In short, we latch onto what is familiar because we are fearful of the unknown or doubtful that anything better could come our way. Holding tight manifests as the controlling and manipulating behavior of self and others, usually by means of guilt or fear. Key phrase: "doubting life".

These three behaviors of ego are important to pay close attention to as recognizing them will lead to great success in shifting your own egoic patterning. Additionally, as you will see from the "negative" manifestation of each behavior, our often unconscious (unmindful), ego (delusional) thinking equates to a lot of pain for ourselves and others.

Delusional Thinking:

As you will surely notice throughout this book, I use the word "illusion" frequently. Illusion simply refers to thinking that is not grounded in present reality — often filled with assumption, opinion, and storytelling based on emotional perspectives. We are programmed biologically to think... and to do so constantly. However, when left unchecked, our thoughts become our worst enemies because we all too often use our mental energy to rehash the past, worry about the present, and overanalyze scenarios of the future. Additionally, when we add in the Push, Pull, and Hold Tight concepts — we can begin to fully see just how egotistical and self-centered our minds (or Self) really are. In short, we create much unnecessary mental and emotional — and even physical — pain for ourselves and others when we let our insecurities dictate our behaviors.

Another Way to Approach Our Egos

Reverse Push: Calm Acceptance

Anger and judgmental attitudes stem from hard and fast opinions about things that we may deem wrong or bad. We see something we don't like, and we are ready to go to war. W.A.R. = We Are Right! However, 99% of the time we don't need to have an opinion about what's going on outside ourselves or in anyone else's life. Instead, we can just accept people and situations as they are.

Exception: Sometimes, we must stand up and speak out on behalf of the wellbeing of others. We can stand in our strength and speak from a place of peace rather than one of violence or anger. Our natural, calm demeanor will promote clearer communication channels — a definite advantage. Make no mistake, being calm and confident isn't the same as being silent and insecure. Both attitudes may appear quiet, but the second actually weakens us, while the first, the ability to speak with peaceful dignity, exudes incredible power. Never mistake calmness for weakness! A calm mind is self-contained while a turbulent mind is easily manipulated. Anger is like a carrot hung from a stick in front of a donkey — point the donkey in any direction and it will follow the carrot, and the same is true of the way we can blindly follow our emotional impulses in the heat of emotion.

Reverse Pull: Accept & Let Go

We all hear stories of people chasing their dreams and achieving their happy endings; however, we're rarely told that it's not really "happily ever after". Sure, they may have reached their goal or personal landmark, but getting what they want has nothing to do with actual happiness or life satisfaction. What immediately happens is that another goal is set, and then another, then another. The chase never ends because the ego always wants more.

Even if we eat the best meal of our lives, shortly thereafter we will be hungry again. Even if we begin making more money than we dreamed possible—we'll still have to manage it properly and then worry about maintaining the lifestyle having it entails. Even if we have our dream wedding and create our dream family—we will incessantly worry about everyone's health and wellbeing because death and loss of those we love is inevitable. We will always be chasing some new idea, some greater feeling, some further goal, some ultimate peace… unless we let go of thinking we need pleasure, need to feel secure, or need to feel loved to be happy. We can have pleasure, security, and love—but these three things, if we are attached to them and fear losing them, will forever keep a gnawing goblin camped out in the back of our mind.

There is nothing "wrong" or "bad" with having goals; the primary wisdom of this teaching is simply that we are invited to recognize and embrace the impermanence of everything— accept the temporary. The stress we cause ourselves with our constant searching, questing, and wanting everything to be a certain way before we can allow ourselves to feel happy and at peace is an illusion that we need not feed into. Instead, we can learn to live our life today, not tomorrow, and cultivate grace and dignity in everything we do imperfectly in the present rather than waiting for some moment when everything fits together perfectly. Plot twist: that moment never comes. Peace is born of accepting the fact that everything in existence falls apart and falls into place, only to then fall apart again. Everything is in constant flux. There's no firm ground to stand upon, and that is genuinely okay. This is how our impermanent lives were made to be. Grasping for anything solid in external sources of validation is the greatest illusion of all.

Reverse Hold: Acceptance & Release

What is shared about impermanence in Reverse Pull also beautifully echoes as true for Reverse Hold.

We are so afraid of the shaky ground beneath our feet that we do some incredibly hurtful things to ourselves and others just to keep our falling house of cards together. We often spend our entire lives struggling to hold onto something that we feel we need—a marriage, a relationship, a job, an identity—yet the effort makes us miserable every single day.

Why do we do this? On the surface, we *think* we do it because it's the "right" thing to do, but ultimately, in the deepest corners of our subconscious minds, we really do it because we're terrified. We're terrified to be alone for the first time in our lives, possibly, or we believe we're unlovable, worthless, or a bad person. Secretly, we believe all the awful things people have said to us repeatedly in the past—or still say to us, as in cases of harmful relationships. How do we know this to be true? Because the only people who permit other people to speak cruelly to them are the ones who (in part or full) *do* believe that what is being said about them is true, and thus, unknowingly perpetuate the abusive behavior.

Accepting and releasing our need to hold onto anything — be it relationships, physical items, reputations, outdated beliefs and ideas, or even jobs and the roles we play in life — is the ultimate freedom. Now, this doesn't mean we release every obligation and throw caution to the wind, it just means we stop trying to control and manipulate in an attempt to hold something together (or keep someone in our lives) that is so clearly NOT FOR US.

This may be the hardest of the three behaviors of ego to master because it asks us to be brave, even when facing the unknown. Our lives may be in complete disarray without any ground to stand firm upon, and that is okay. What we learn from Reverse Hold is that we can still behave with grace, dignity, and respect towards ourselves and others no matter our circumstances, even when we have nothing left to give. By calmly accepting all of life, letting go of control, and releasing our need to feel safe, secure, loved, and validated — we come to taste the wisdom of the final tenet taught in *Living Peace*: Release Self. But to start, let's begin with the first tenet: Mastery of Thought…

Tenet One:

Mastery of Thought

Flashback:

School, when I was a preteen, was not always a safe place for me. I loved to learn, yet I was socially awkward and always had a different perception of reality than the other kids. Mix that with my passive, "do no harm" mentality, I was the perfect prey for the other kids to project their insecurities and pain onto.

These days, too many young kids commit suicide, and I'll admit that if my parents hadn't acted when they did and switched me to a different school, I could easily have been one of those kids. I was relentlessly abused every day – physically, verbally, and emotionally – and the smile that once lit my face eventually faded away as hollow eyes in an emotionless expression took its place.

*There is a breaking point when kids lose all hope and start to believe the negative reality their peers force onto them. "Maybe I AM worthless. Maybe I AM unlovable. Maybe the world would be better off without me. Maybe I shouldn't exist at all…" Our human minds can only take so much until they start believing in the subtle yet constant whispers of prejudice and hatred that slowly chip away at our self-esteem. However, I was fortunate. Before my inner flame was **completely** extinguished, I found a way to feed the fire of my heart so that it burned brightly once again.*

Between the ages of fourteen and sixteen, I began reading and researching different spiritual and philosophical approaches to life. I read somewhere that I could be the master of my life and I had the power to control my thoughts. This newfound awareness struck the match and lit the little bit of kindling that remained in the nether regions of my mind. The small flame illuminated the knowledge that "I AM beautiful. I AM worthy and deserving of love. I AM important. I HAVE purpose. I LOVE life, and LIFE loves me."

I awoke from my slumber and began to remember the mission I'd been sent into this life to accomplish. I began reconditioning my subconscious mind and turning my life around through positive thinking. No longer did I play this game of life by someone else's rulebook. I stopped going to therapy, which wasn't helping, and stopped taking all my prescriptions for depression, OCD, and anxiety. It was obvious that the only person who really knew what was best for me was me. At just sixteen, I decided to take full responsibility for my happiness and success in life. Two years later, I was crowned the first openly gay prom king at my high school, proving to myself and others that anyone can change their stars.

Mastering our thoughts can only be achieved after we truly understand what reality is. So, it is now time to shatter your pre-conceived concept of reality. The majority of what you perceive as reality exists only in your mind, and, chances are, you spend most of the hours of your life in this illusion. Let me repeat, if it didn't sink in the first time: **The majority of what you perceive as reality exists ONLY IN YOUR MIND,** and, chances are, you spend most of the hours of your life in this ILLUSION. Let's dive deeper into what that means.

Reality is based upon perception, and every single one of us perceives differently, thus, each of us is experiencing a different reality from all others. There are as many realities co-existing in this present moment as there are people alive in this present moment. Who is right? Who is wrong? The answer is irrelevant because duality is also an illusion, since "rightness" and "wrongness" are subjective to the observer. Every single person creates his or her reality based on his or her own perceptions. And each of our realities is made up primarily of illusion because most of us are not living in the present moment.

Let me further explain illusion beyond what we discussed in the last chapter. Comprehension will come much easier if you first understand what illusion is *not*. Illusion is *not* the present moment. The present moment is all that exists, ever. Once a moment has passed, it becomes the past, and any thought spent on the past is dwelling in illusion. Yes, something may have actually happened and was reality, once upon a time; however, projecting ourselves into the past via our thoughts and memories only creates distorted, fragmented reflections of what once was, based on our limited perceptions in the here and now.

Projecting into the future and forming speculations about it is also illusion. Any thoughts about the future — be it a minute from now, a day from now, or ten years from now — are all illusory. Every future reality we concern ourselves with, whether done so with hopefulness and excitement or anxiety and fear, always differs from our expectations once we reach the present moment of it.

Assuming we can predict the realities of other people or situations in the present moment are also illusions. For example, imagining my home while I am at work may very well be thinking in the present timeframe, but thinking about home keeps me from being fully present in my current reality, which is work. Home is illusion, because as I think about it, I'm assuming it to be exactly as I left it, yet in truth, I do not know if it even exists as I left it — since I am not there experiencing it firsthand.

Another example is focusing obsessively on someone else's thoughts and feelings: Do they like me? Are they mad at me? What can I do to influence the way they feel about me? This mind trap is certainly one rabbit hole we've all likely fallen down before. Have you ever spent a day worrying about someone else's behavior towards you only to discover eventually that their actions weren't even about you? Although it's an excellent practice to check in with people any time we notice something is a bit "off" — it is never to our health or benefit to lose our peace by concerning ourselves with assumptions and speculations over the lives and opinions of others.

People often spend most of their waking thoughts obsessing about the past, future, or some other present timeframe situation than the one they are in right now. Therefore, most people spend the majority of their lives living in delusional projections and fantasy storytelling. It is these illusions that also create the realities of separation they experience because of becoming emotionally attached to these mental projections and expectations. After all, only the present moment contains life, as illustrated in the example below:

As the busy mom drives her kids to school each morning, she thinks about what she must accomplish in the day and feels the stress of it all while driving, rendering her unable to be fully present in the moment with her children. She half listens to them every day because she's so wrapped up in the things she must later do. She feels distanced from her kids because of this, so she tries to squeeze in more one-on-one time with them. Yet when they do spend time together in other settings, she's still not fully present, so the closeness and peace of mind she seeks is never achieved.

All of this could be resolved if the mom lived in the present moment and realized driving with her kids is all that exists in that moment. Thinking and worrying about what must be done during the day will not help her get those things done more quickly or efficiently. And so, when she is with her kids, she is *with* her kids—fully present and feeling good about it, happy, and close to them. And they feel the same.

Although it may be hard to believe at first, living in the present moment actually **adds** time to the day, since we utilize the present moment for all that its worth and focus on the task at hand with full attention instead of distraction. When we are mindful, we feel good, and when we feel good, we get things done more quickly and with greater efficiency. When we are stressed, we feel distant, we produce shoddier work; it's easy to get frustrated and manifest setbacks, it becomes harder to embrace joy, and our general satisfaction in life decreases — all of which decreases the time we have each day ("Where did the time go?" we ask!). To live does not mean simply going through the motions; we only truly *live* when we embrace each moment with full awareness. Again, only the present moment contains life.

Have you ever recalled a memory that caused you actual physical pain — perhaps an anxious gnawing in your gut? And what happens when you think about a potentially stressful situation you expect to go through? It's amazing that our thoughts can create such very real physical reactions in our bodies, so much so, that they are equal to the sensations we'd be experiencing if we were actually going through the past or future in the present moment. Yet we aren't. It's pure illusion. **Illusions can and do create PHYSICAL Dis-Ease in our bodies.** So, it's most important to master our thoughts, to become cognizant of what we are spending our precious mental energy on each and every moment of every day. Are our thoughts uplifting us, or are they dimming us down?

It's essential to point out that illusions aren't necessarily "bad" things. And, as I mentioned before, there is no duality here. It's all about which direction feels better when embraced. Put simply, "negative" means separating energies, while "positive" means unifying energies. As an analogy, imagine two people's hearts either drifting further away from the other, or being drawn closer. This feeling of connection or disconnection is what happens whenever we have positive or negative thoughts. Though illusion, in and of itself, isn't "negative", it does feel better to go in the direction of unifying energies. Yet, all too often, when we get into illusion, we jump to worst-case scenario thinking.

For example, when someone cuts us off while driving, why do so many of us automatically think the worst about the driver, often actually cursing them? We don't know what's going on in their reality, so a negative projection on them is as much an illusion as a positive projection would be. However, thinking positively and creating a compassionate story as the reason why they cut us off would actually make us feel better. If we're going to be in illusion, we might as well make it a positive one! Therefore, whenever we're experiencing a stressful situation, using positive illusion can bring us peace of mind and relaxation.

An important disclaimer!

As you progress in your practice, the goal is to eventually, drop all assumptive storytelling — both positive and negative. We learn that we simply don't need to make up a story or have a dualistic opinion about most, if not all, things. Our strength instead derives from observing our life factually and objectively — taking action when necessary and not carrying the weight of a troubled mind when situations are outside our realm of influence. We peacefully release our attachments and resistance while resisting telling stories that are illusory just to make our egos feel better. This is an advanced approach that may take time to fully embody. Nonetheless, please keep the importance of "releasing all stories" at the forefront of your mind as something to work towards, even if you choose to start by substituting positive illusions first. After all, if we can't imagine our lives becoming better, they never will get better — thus, positive illusion is still a powerful step to begin with!

Reality creation through the imagination of positive illusion is a critical tool in shifting the direction of people's thoughts, and hence, their lives. **Always remember: action follows thought**, or rather, **action follows belief** — which stems from thought. Our daily behavior changes drastically whether our mind is full of doubt or filled with confidence. However, both doubt and confidence become obsolete once we achieve consistent inner peace. As we dive into later tenets this perpetual mindset and stance of neutrality and objectivity will begin to make more and more sense.

Note: Another powerful teaching to understand is that there actually is no such thing as doubt! Doubt is placing our complete certainty (confidence) into something that doesn't feel good, i.e. we are **certain** *that we're not good enough; we are* **certain** *we're unlovable, we are* **certain** *we will fail, we are* **certain** *other people will break our trust. Therefore, removing and transcending the chains of doubt is a matter of changing one's perspective and singular focus of opinion.*

The story I shared at the beginning of this chapter — of my younger self overcoming insecurity and low self-esteem — is a great example of how a shift in focus can completely change our experienced reality. No-thing changes, yet everything becomes different. The shift is purely internal, proving just how much power our mind has over the lives we live and create for ourselves.

Exploring Affirmations

Most people are duped into thinking that their negative illusions are close friends because they mistake their thoughts and feelings as factual reality. That's why positive affirmations are so important. Affirmations are positive conscious thoughts used to recondition and purge our subconscious minds of our negative beliefs, which we will explore more deeply in *Practice 1: The File Exchange.*

Beliefs are positive or negative thoughts that have turned

into positive or negative expectations of reality. They aren't set in stone, yet many people treat them as if they are. A negative expectation of reality is a form of **negative self-certainty.** We become so certain of our negative emotion or perceived negative situation that we are unable to see anything beyond it. This is where the adage of, "don't make a permanent decision based upon a temporary emotion", comes into play. Expectations and negative self-certainty are something we'll explore in greater depth under the heading of Vibrational Expectations in the *Ignorance is an Illusion* chapter, while emotional discernment and self-control will be taught in the *Mastery of Emotion* chapter.

Advanced Teachings on Mastery of Thought:

Mastery of thought is better achieved when we understand what illusion is and how our perceptions create "reality".

Our ability to perceive life with our six senses creates only the foundation of the reality we experience. What is then built on that foundation is entirely our choice. As mentioned previously, the majority of our experienced reality is primarily constructed of illusion. It's all subjective, and every individual has a different perception of life that each of us views through our own lenses. This means there are as many realities co-existing simultaneously in this present moment as there are people alive on the planet.

The most frequently asked question then becomes, "What is reality, then, since most — if not everything — we deem to be true is actually some form of a projected illusion?" And the answer is, "Reality is (mostly) what we make it to be." That's what's so exciting about mastering our thoughts. If our reality is created by our perceptions, and all perceptions are illusions, then life itself is an illusion that we can adjust in our mind to create an experience that better serves us. Let me give an example to clarify this:

There are as many "Alaric Hutchinsons" as there are people perceiving me, since no one can experience me the same way another does. To illustrate: in my field of work, people have perceived me as a wise man. Yet, when I interact with people who have no understanding or interest in what I do, they may think my teachings are nonsense and I am foolish.

Am I wise? Am I a fool? There is no singular answer here. Each person's reality is personal to them, so their created reality of me is also "accurate" for them. In fact, who I am matters very little to the observer since they can only perceive me to the limited extent of their own mental and emotional bias. Truly fascinating! Every person who has ever interacted with me has a different picture of me in his or her mind. And when they bring to conscious thought my face and energy, each person will call into being an Alaric that is in resonance with their personal bias and vibrational aura.

Vibrational reality:

Our realities are created through our perceptions, and our perceptions are hued by our vibrations (collective energies of thoughts, feelings, and emotions). A joyous person who is grateful in life will find the divinity even in the cruelest person, while an unhappy, cynical person will find the flaws and criticize even the holiest of saints. Perception is based on the observer's vibration—not on the vibration of the object, situation, or person being observed. Note: the later chapter of *Explaining Vibrational Aura* will better define this concept.

All of this is important to understand because we want to shatter the brittle beliefs that reality is set in stone and that it is more physical than mental. Reality is more **MENTAL** than physical. The physical circumstances of our lives matter very little, while the thoughts, perceptions, and belief systems we create *about* the physical matter greatly.

When we believe that the physical is all there is, and that life is only what is in front of us; that we were dealt a bad hand of cards and we're stuck with that hand for the rest of our lives — well, that "negative" expectation becomes our belief system which turns into a never-ending "reality" of suffering. And all along it was just the illusion of negative self-certainty.

Perception alters reality — or rather, **perception creates a MENTAL OVERLAY onto the physical landscape of reality.** What this means is that everything we experience in life is neutral. Let me repeat that: **Everything we experience in life is neutral.** It is our MIND, or rather our egoic mind, that projects its MENTAL OVERLAY, or hue, that colors life — and often not for the better. Rather than seeing all things as neutral, we compartmentalize, label, and judge. Eventually, our mental overlay (personal perception) acts as a biased filter that sifts through each of our experiences — letting in information that our ego agrees with while blocking anything that's disagreeable. This subconscious behavior is especially dangerous regarding things we don't like, as it allows less and less of the full richness of LIFE to reach our awareness.

Remember the 5 Layers of Consciousness? This Mental Overlay is what keeps people trapped in the Mundane and Collective. Our experienced reality becomes solely based upon the filtered perceptions (often illusions) that we become attached to and call factual reality. This is why Mastery of Thought is so crucial; it helps us break free of the cycle of our self-created "limbos" and "hells" while giving us the mental prowess necessary to create a life of beauty and peace.

When we shift our thoughts about the world around us in the other direction, our earthly circumstances begin to change. A curse turns into a blessing. A painful experience turns into a powerful lesson. A "sinner" finds redemption. A once miserable life turns into one full of hope and opportunity.

Practice 1
The File Exchange
(Mastery of Thought)

It is of the utmost importance that you are able to begin to distinguish between delusion & reality — meaning, discerning what is actual, tangible truth and what is your own emotional and mental bias. An easy way to remember this is: ALL OPINION is egoic illusion. Opinion is not truth, and therefore it is a projection of your own thoughts, feelings, emotions, and the collective experiences that bias your intake of information (often towards the negative).

Thoughts: Files (conscious mind)
Beliefs: Filing Cabinet (subconscious mind)

Throughout our lives, we accumulate thoughts that, over time, are ingrained in our subconscious minds and become beliefs. Imagine it as piling up files (thoughts) that we then store away in filing cabinets, each cabinet representing a different aspect of our experienced life and psyche. And once a cabinet is full, it is labeled by our ego to become a default belief that, when triggered, ignites an emotional reaction. We do not experience emotion unless a belief is triggered to sway the direction of our emotions in some way. And even though the files were stacked in our subconscious minds without our direct awareness, once we become aware of them, we are able to sort through and replace the ones that no longer serve us with new, self-chosen files that do serve us. This is the power behind positive affirmations; they are among the files that recondition the mind.

Positive Affirmation is a way to take back control of your mental faculties, especially in the subconscious mind. In more esoteric teachings this practice is called "self-suggestion" or "autosuggestion".

When something or someone triggers an emotional reaction or judgment in us, we know that there's a belief involved. It is as if a file from the cabinet comes flying out and slaps us in the face. Through mindful practice and cultivated self-awareness, we can use positive affirmations to catch the thought (flying file), delete it because it's outdated, and replace it with an updated, positive-thought file.

Over time, with consistent effort, we can directly sort out all "negative" files in a cabinet and replace them with positive thought files. Once this task of sorting is completed, whatever negative belief we were working on changes. For example, a subconscious belief (filing cabinet) filled with low self-esteem thoughts will be filled with their positives and relabeled as High Self-esteem Thoughts.

Examples of reconditioning in the Layers of Consciousness:

Mundane Consciousness Thoughts:
  ➤ *Day in and day out people continue to disappoint me.*
  ➤ *I blame people for disappointing me — it's their fault.*

Becoming **Collective Consciousness** Thoughts:
  ➤ *People disappointment sometimes, but I quickly forgive them.*
  ➤ *When I feel disappointment, I try to remember that everyone is doing the best they can with what they know.*

Becoming **Transcendent Consciousness** Thoughts:
  ➤ *It's my own expectations that create my disappointment, and I understand that no one has the power to disappointment me unless I give them that power.*
  ➤ *My disappointment in others is often a mirror of the disappointment I feel in myself.*

Becoming **Galactic Consciousness** Thoughts:
> ➢ *I am superbly grateful for any spontaneous feeling of disappointment that arises within me, for it shows me areas of my life that I have yet to make peace.*
> ➢ *I am beyond grateful for every interaction I have – thank you, thank you, thank you!*

Becoming **Cosmic Consciousness** Thoughts:
> ➢ *All is well, all is well, and all is most beautifully well!*

As you can see in the above reconditioning examples, there are multiple layers of options to choose from. Use this as your guide to help discern where you are at on your path and which Layer of Consciousness you may be residing in. Please note that it is not recommended to immediately jump from Mundane to Galactic or Cosmic as it is important for your egoic mind to first agree with the new affirmations you are working with—otherwise it may feel like you are lying to yourself. Please also ensure that your affirmations and adopted new beliefs always make logical sense – do not just regurgitate positive affirmations because you've read them in a book and then committed them to memory. Explore your affirmations and find ways in which they apply to your life and are valid.

For example, the "all is well" affirmation makes perfect sense to me, and I can explain its wisdom very clearly to anyone. Yet, often, when I have new students, their egos are too ready and eager to spout out a million reasons why things are NOT at all well! Aware of this, I certainly do not teach them that affirmation to start with. Instead, I choose something they may find easier to swallow.

It may be helpful to make a list of your most negative beliefs (thoughts you think repeatedly about yourself, others, or the world each day). Make a chart with five categories, one for each layer of consciousness, then write our your "negative" thoughts in whatever category seems most appropriate. You can also do this with other thoughts you have, even neutral and positive ones, since they may still, more subtly, show room for growth.

A helpful guide:

Mundane = blaming and criticizing thoughts
Collective = softly judgmental yet forgiving thoughts
Transcendent = self-aware and self-responsibility thoughts
Galactic = grateful thoughts
Cosmic = no analysis and genuine wellness of peace thoughts

The Practice

Whenever you have "negative" thoughts or judgments about yourself, other people, or any situation, this is your opportunity to use the File Exchange exercise to replace the negative thought with a positive thought. It will take time, consistency, and repetition to accomplish. In the past, whenever I had a negative thought about myself or someone else, I would repeat a positive affirmation over and over again in my head until I forgot about the judgment. Over time, my default reactions toward life became optimistic and hopeful, rather than automatically thinking thoughts that were pessimistic, cynical, and didn't make me feel good.

Remember, it's our job to feel "well" every day, and that there is never a reason good enough to be out of alignment with peace. It is our alignment with peace and feeling good that allows us to manifest our best reality here on Earth. When we are in fear, judgment, or experiencing any form of negative thought or emotion, we are lowering our vibration and exuding it outward, dimming our lights and casting shadows on those around us.

Using the File Exchange and shifting our thoughts is the first step to being masters of our lives. When our minds are on autopilot, our focus goes from shiny thing to shiny thing, unaware that the shiny thing may not be for our highest benefit and may actually be attracting "negative" energy into our lives. When we are in control of our minds, we gain the ability to pick and choose what we wish to be manifested into our lives. The mind is our greatest the tool for creation. Some say we are using it to activate and direct the Universal Law of Attraction.

Disclaimer:

Results with this practice of file exchange can take a very long time to see if we don't keep at it consistently. For example, there are tens of thousands of thoughts we think each day — so reconditioning just a couple dozen thoughts in the morning or evening isn't going to cut it! We are called to remain mindful throughout the day, using the File Exchange upwards of a few hundred times, not just a few times. Additionally, if we skip a day or two, the mindful work we previously put in will likely have been replaced once again by negative thoughts and self-criticisms — thus we cannot simply start where we left off. Instead, it's best to start our mental reconditioning practice over completely, or at least add on a few more days of consistent practice.

I say all of this not to discourage you from the File Exchange. I wish to give you a necessary perspective to adopt and a reason why you may not be seeing results if you happen to be very casual about applying the practice. If you want powerful results, you must keep this practice in the forefront of your mind each day for several weeks instead of lackadaisically using it on a whim or only half the time when judgments start creeping in.

It is recommended to set a goal for yourself ranging from one to four weeks, keeping track of the days with a 2:1 ratio anytime you skip a day. Thus, if you skip one day of practice, add two more days to your set goal.

Eventually, this practice will become second nature for you, and it won't call for such diligent self-discipline. When your thoughts are predominantly positive or neutral, then a regular morning or evening routine used for residue judgments and to keep one's mind clear of complaints or negative storytelling will suffice. The *Counting Gratitudes* practice taught alongside tenet eight is a beautiful evolution of the File Exchange, helping you to maintain your inner peace as a continued practice for years to come.

Examples of everyday thought reconditioning

"I don't like myself." / "I hate myself."
  ➤ *I don't need to have an opinion about myself*
  ➤ *I choose to love and accept myself.*
  ➤ *I love and accept myself.*

"I'm stupid." / "I can't do anything right." / "I'm a failure."
  ➤ *Each day I choose to continue learning and bettering myself.*
  ➤ *Like the lives of everyone else, my life has worth and purpose.*

"If people get to know the real me, they won't like me."
  ➤ *I love and accept myself; therefore, it doesn't matter if other people choose not to see my kindness and worth.*
  ➤ *It's okay if people get to know the "real" me and don't like what they see or hear. By living authentically free, I will attract new people into my life who will accept and love me for me.*

"People are stupid and annoying."
  ➤ *Everyone is doing the best they can with what they know.*

> ➤ *Other people probably think my judgments are stupid and annoying — How ironic! I choose instead to foster compassion and a light heart towards humanity's foibles!*

"I don't trust anyone."
> ➤ *Every day, I choose to open my heart just a little bit more.*
> ➤ *I trust in myself and my own peace; therefore, I can handle other people's attempts at trust, even when things don't work out and lead to pain.*

"Humans are awful." / "Our planet is doomed."
> ➤ *Even amidst a planet in conflict, I choose to share peace.*
> ➤ *Humans are like children learning to walk for the first time, yet, as adults, this means they are learning to live in peace with each other. I release my judgments and choose to help where I can rather than add to the separation.*

Tenet Two:
Mastery of Impulse

Flashback:

The angst of my adolescent years of depression was exacerbated greatly by my Obsessive/Compulsive Disorder. The worst symptom was excessive hand washing. I washed them so often, my hands would begin to crack and bleed, and still, they didn't feel clean. I also had multiple impulsive tics, and often had to complete them in sets of three with a final big one to top off the previous set of three. If I didn't feel satisfied with how they came off, I would repeat them again and again until I felt they were complete. An example of this was the popping sound I would make with my mouth, or the twitching of my eyebrow. If I was unable to finish the set of tics, or worse yet, if I couldn't wash my hands when I felt the urge, my body would tense up in extreme stress that sometimes morphed into panic attacks. I can only liken the power of these feelings to wanting to pull my hair out and tear my flesh off. It was as though I wanted to destroy my own body in order to escape.

Most of the time, my OCD didn't interfere too much with everyday life. The extreme panic attacks only occurred when I felt under overwhelming stress at home and in school. Once I removed myself from all medications when I was sixteen and began to study Eastern methods of mastering impulse through meditation, I realized that the impulsive tics I had weren't real, even though my body felt as though it would go berserk if I didn't satisfy the urges. Each time a compulsion arose, I pushed the sensations of my body aside and focused on training my mind, repeating mantras such as: "I am in control." "I do not need to do this to feel complete." "I am complete as I am." "This feeling will pass." "Everything is temporary, including this urge." "I am the master of my mind and body." Then I'd sit on my hands and continue to deep breathe, repeating the mantras in my head until the moment passed. Generally, this took between one and five minutes. The urges grew less frequent as the years went on, and the OCD became nearly nonexistent in my life. To this day, I do still have a couple of quirks, but they are no longer tics that cause me stress if I don't allow them to control me. I took back the power of my life using breathing techniques, meditation, and relevant mantras.

Mastery of Impulse encourages us to develop greater self-discipline and cultivate willpower so that we may be in better control of our impulses, which then allows us to more consciously choose how we interact with life. Please note, however, that one must have at least some awareness and skill with *Mastery of Thought* for Mastery of Impulse to occur. Without the foundation of mindfulness taught in the previous tenet, our ability to further cultivate self-discipline over our impulsive and addictive tendencies may be met with great challenge. If at any point you find yourself struggling with Mastery of Impulse, it is of worth to revisit *Mastery of Thought* and apply another wave of the File Exchange practice to your life.

At this stage in our human evolution, we still tend to run on habits of impulse, habits of desire, and habits of comfort. We react, we crave, and we avoid discomfort and embarrassment at all costs. The cost, however, is our inability to be self-aware and exercise self-control.

In our desire to heighten or dull our senses, we avoid the uncomfortable truths that have nudged our consciences over our lifetime. This is how people end up in relationships as the abuser or abused and stay in them for years, how people fall into and die of addiction, and in a general sense, how people simply stop feeling peace and joy (or possibly never have). All this pain stems from the inability to discipline our mental, emotional, and physical behavior.

Note, however, that very few of us are ever efficiently taught *how* to discipline ourselves in a positive way. We may have been disciplined and taught how to follow rules;

however, that is not the same as **self**-discipline. Most of us probably understand discipline in its negative connotation, such as punishment or censure when we do not meet set expectations. This criticizing approach to discipline often causes us to have an aversion to the word, and further propagates its misuse and/or underuse.

Habits of impulse, desire, and comfort all fulfill one goal: satisfying the ego.

To cultivate self-discipline, we must begin surrendering our egos to our higher awareness (some may say God). This is done by "getting over ourselves" and doing things that we don't necessarily want to do. We begin putting stillness and peace before our habits of impulse, abstinence and sobriety before our habits of desire, and uncomfortable yet strengthening routines before our comforting habits. For example, sitting on the floor meditating is rarely comfortable at first — and our ego says, "I don't need to do this!" and so we stop. Self-discipline is following through, even when the ego urges us to give up.

Continuing to build on the last tenet, impulse control — or impulse awareness — is of the utmost importance when it comes to catching our thoughts before they turn into regrettable words, actions, or life-altering decisions.

Humans have the tendency to react when stimulated by some outside force, often feeling "triggered" (frightened, hurt, insulted, disrespected, etc.). Now that we are aware that what we think and feel is not necessarily true, this understanding helps us cool the fires of our impulsiveness when interacting with others. The inability to be introspective is what keeps them trapped in their negative emotional continuums. Thus, it is vitally important that we continuously reflect on why we feel the way we do, and where these feelings come from (within).

It's never of benefit to react with a "knee-jerk" impulse because such a response is always a temporary uprising that often later leads to the expansion of negative feelings such as guilt or shame, especially if we acted rashly in our heightened emotions. By catching our impulsive tendencies — choosing to consciously shift them so that we speak from a place of peace, reason, and compassion — we break the cycle and begin to create a different reality for ourselves, free from unconsciously reproducing the same problems day after day.

Often, people in the Mundane or Collective Consciousness use justifications to explain why they can't be in control of their own lives or the impulsive behaviors that repeatedly cause them pain. It's quite ironic that our culture has adopted the belief that the majority of us are just not "wired" right and therefore are unable to take responsibility for their lives. So many of the labels that were once used to help identify and overcome an issue have now become lifelong crutches that limit us from doing certain things. In truth, only a very small percentage of people actually fall into the category of not being able to overcome their "labeled issue" and live full and happy lives. The wonderful news is that if you are aware enough to read and understand this book, you have the cognitive ability to take control of your life and develop peace of mind, body, and soul.

I invite you to release all labels you have — those others have given you, and those you've given yourself. No more self-identifying Dis-Eases, addictions, mental or physical illnesses, social anxiety setbacks, damaged childhoods, turbulent past stories, stressful lives, peer or family pressure, etc., etc., etc. None of these matter right now, in this moment. NOW, there is no more recounting your victim story, and there are no more "can'ts". There is no more "it's too hard," and there are no more justifications. You played your last excuse card years ago, and you're done making them.

Why is this so important? Because you must challenge your preconceived notions (beliefs) about yourself so that new information and experiences can come into your life. Never allow yourself to be trapped in self-fulfilling prophesies! In short: **we get what we expect!**

Now, I'm not asking you to throw away your medications or revisit past addictions — I'm just asking you to release the story of why you feel you can't have peace or develop self-control. If you truly believe you're not capable of being the victor of your life, then the battle is already lost. It doesn't matter who anyone is, what your past was, or what your current issue is — if you want to find peace and be happy, it *is* possible. And, again, if you are cognitive enough to read this book, you do possess the mental ability to develop strong self-control, willpower, and mindfulness — all of which are necessary to develop peace in life. Let today be the day you decide to take back the power and control over your life. The time is now, and it starts with making that choice and sticking to it.

Sometimes people feel the need to react or yell in anger because their calm speech falls on deaf ears — but they must ask themselves, what result does anger bring? Anger may motivate, but it also kills inspiration and burns bridges of communication. It is important to understand that it is not enough to simply speak calmly; we must also practice compassionate listening and the freedom to disagree without interruption.

Mastery of Impulse is also relevant when it comes to addictive tendencies. Negative reaction is indeed a form of addiction, possibly the greatest addiction humans have, but let's explore the other external addictions more deeply. The root of most addictions is a desire to escape pain or a reality of perceived constant suffering. What starts off as a way to escape our pain and bring relief eventually becomes the very activity that traps us in our suffering. Without acknowledging and embracing what is causing us pain, we cannot learn from it or transform it. We continue to impulsively avoid what bothers us.

Those who are patient are able to create and change their reality because they allow room for pause in their lives. Most addictions tend to flare up during times of aloneness because subconscious, painful thoughts and memories surface when there's no external stimulation to distract us from them. Those who do not make time for stillness in their lives continue to avoid these moments, while those who have learned patience use this time, no matter how painful it may be, to explore their minds and turn their suffering into useful information. This information then becomes fertilizer to help them grow. Embracing pain becomes easier and easier to do as we learn that pain is not bad, nor is it an enemy. Pain is necessary for our conscious growth, and when we embrace it, we start the process of healing our emotional impulsiveness, mental and physical reactions, and physical addictions.

Further Exploring Addition & Avoidist Behavior

The root cause of all addiction is a combination of neurosis (delusion) and a desire to not feel and face our pain. Once upon a time, in a stressful or unhappy moment, we reached for something or someone to take the "edge off". Addiction occurred when we kept going back to that source of temporary satisfaction or relief even after it was no longer needed, and so created a dependency.

We all have addictions; they just vary in degree. Whether we are in heavily into addiction or not, we all have ways by which we distract ourselves from being fully alive and present each day, and in very subtle ways this behavior damages our relationships and ability to achieve goals.

Some terms to keep in mind as we continue are:

Addiction: a developed dependency for relief or pleasure
Avoidism: subconscious or conscious denial of reality
Escapism: subconscious or conscious rejection of reality
Distraction: any combination of the above three used to numb pain or discomfort

Note: Each of the above is a form of neurosis caused by egoic delusion and a fear of pain. No matter how much physical or situational pain and discomfort we may feel, we must learn to not run away from it. Pain is not bad or wrong — it's simply information that's here to teach us, thus, it's important never to let it go to waste!

Over the years, I have worked with many people who struggled with addictions. The core wisdom each learned that allowed them to heal their addiction was facing their unresolved emotional wounds. Often what kept them in addiction and avoidist behavior was fear of pain — fear that if they fully let all the hurt in, they wouldn't be able to keep functioning, or possibly they wouldn't even want to live because the weight of the pain was too great.

However, not everyone has a major addiction with overwhelming guilt and shame attached to it — some of us are merely "functioning escapists" who keep ourselves impulsively distracted enough to skate on the surface of life rather than plunging into the depths of the subconscious muck that makes us uneasy and insecure. Whatever our degree of addiction or avoidist behavior, it still traps us in suffering because — even when we may feel "high" from a "substance": physical pleasure, eating, shopping, or even chasing spiritual elation—none brings inner peace. All are fleeting, a perfume masking the stench of our mental and emotional "shit".

Sometimes, it's just too painful to fully accept what we have done or what someone else has done to us. This Earth can be a violent place. Even so, this doesn't justify "going to sleep at the wheel" and allowing the "car crash" of our behavior to negatively impact everyone around us. If we continue to "drive recklessly", we will be sucked into a downward spiral. We begin hating ourselves for hurting those closest to us because of our addictions or avoidist behavior, so then we turn to the addiction even more to take the edge off and escape our growing pain, which makes us feel even worse, and hit the "substance" even harder. It becomes a vicious cycle, indeed. However, it can cease once we stop running and numbing.

We must face our pain if we are to ever break the cycle of impulsiveness that manifests as addictive, aggressive, and avoidist behaviors.

Embracing our pain will hurt, but that's okay. Accept that it will hurt so you can then begin the healing process. **We cannot heal what we do not acknowledge.** And although acknowledging what we believe are the "worst" parts of ourselves, or the "worst" parts of life can lead to pain, it is only temporary.

I invite you to say out loud the following sentence as you read it: *"By confronting my pain today, I will not have to feel suffering tomorrow."*

The process of confronting our pain is a continuous one. Some days will show more progress than others. Sometimes, just showing up, even when it hurts, is the bravest thing we can do.

As you continue reading, the tenets and practices will become invaluable tools for healing pain and conflict as you advance through the rest of your life.

Practice 2
Pause, Process & Respond
(*Mastery of Impulse*)

It's amazing how just a little bit of awareness can dramatically transform our realities. Throughout our lives, we will find ourselves in contrasting situations that trigger us and make us want to react—often blindly, hastily, and rashly. Consistently being aware of when a pause is needed can make all the difference. This may sound overly simple, so simple that it can easily be dismissed. However, let me explain why a few seconds' pause can make such a dynamic difference.

When faced with contrast, a situation counter to what we desire, we dig in our heels against it, causing a friction that often escalates things. Pausing disrupts the buildup of negative energy by entirely stopping the friction or by decreasing it to a manageable degree, depending on how we respond. Any situation that affects us on an impulse level can only spiral out of control if we give it our energy as a participant. In taking that pause and removing ourselves— however briefly—we can completely shift the direction of the energy. How do we pause? By taking a few deep breaths. The flood of oxygen soothes us, helping our mind and body relax as we encourage rational thinking so that we may better respond with peace.

Most people don't do this, though. Instead, they needlessly perpetuate the drama, conflict, stress, and suffering in their lives. They give into their reactive impulses rather than responding with a clear mind. Living in the present moment allows us to think and respond rationally; however, when we are not present, our attention is divided and the likelihood of reacting rashly is greatly increased.

An example: Most, if not all, of us have certain family members who seem to know the exact location of the buttons to push that can make us explode. We pick up the phone or attend a family gathering, and the conversation turns to our faults or foibles. Buttons pushed, we feel the hot lava that precedes an eruption rise from our bellies to our chests. We become more and more heated as the unthinking, unkind words continue to be spoken, and our tongues begin to bleed from biting them so hard. And finally, when we cannot take anymore, the lava spews out from us in reaction to the most recent button pushed, and a family feud ensues. And sometimes, when we leave the interaction, we dive into a soft or hard addiction to take the edge off, allowing ourselves to unwind. Both of these behaviors, the explosion and the indulging, are forms of impulsive reactions we have when dealing with stress.

Response is crucial because "where our thoughts go energy flows". Whatever words come out of our mouths hold energy, and that energy will either create or perpetuate the peace or drama of our reality. If we want change, it must begin with our thoughts, words, and the focus of our attention before these can be aligned with action. So, we pause by consciously taking deep breaths, taking a moment to process the situation, and then respond with peace. When we come from a place of peace, we are able to bring greater clarity, harmony, and co-creation to the situation, fostering harmony among everyone involved — or at the least not escalating it! The way we respond to the world is the way the world will respond to us. Peace is a choice, and each of us can hone our ability to speak with more peace as we develop greater self-control day by day.

I like to use the example of the time my mom unexpectedly reached out to a cashier in a busy line. It was during the holiday season, and the cashier was in a foul mood, which caused her to fail to give Mom her discount on several purchases. My mom tried to intervene a couple of times, which only made the woman snap at her.

*In the past, Mom would have given the woman a piece of her mind,
but this day she chose another path, instead. She reached over and
clasped the cashier's hand, looked straight into her eyes and asked
her to take a deep breath. She said, "I know this is a stressful time,
but just know that everything always works itself out. Don't worry
about my discount. It's okay. Thank you, and you are loved."*

*The cashier's eyes glossed over with tears and she was speechless.
Mom finished paying and left. She exuberantly recounted the story
to me later that day, happy with the way she'd turned things around
both for herself and for the woman, even though she never got her
discounts.*

Mastery of impulse is all about self-discipline and choice.
The mind is a powerful tool that gives us the ability to be in
control of ourselves. We must cultivate the willpower to use it,
especially since too many of us have been on autopilot for too
long and often tend to focus on the "negative." Furthermore,
when we are on autopilot, we continuously give our inner
power away to others. The unnecessary drama/mundane
grind of our lives saps our strength, removing our magnificent
creative ability to alter and manifest a more enlightened
reality in the living world around us. Having awareness, self-
discipline, and willpower gives us back our power so that we
may channel this energy into benefiting ourselves and those
around us with more peace, co-creation, and unconditional
love.

Exploring the Acronym of PPR:

P: Pause

Any time we feel triggered — triggered meaning whenever
our egoic fight or flight mode kicks in — we pause by
breathing. Our ego (our inner critic and critic of others) wants
to react by saying something rash or rushing to *do* something

(like fighting). Instead, our <u>response-ability</u> is to soothe and quell our incoming "negative" thoughts, feelings, and emotions so they do not take control. Taking a long, deep breath, or multiple deep breaths, interrupts the building momentum, helping us to not react.

Pausing with breath is a beautiful thing. Science has proven that deep breathing has a beneficial impact on our mind and body. Increasing our oxygen intake helps the brain process and think more clearly while it also relaxes our muscles. When we are triggered, our body tenses up and our breathing tends to become shallow. Reversing this tendency to tense up by consciously breathing allows us to break the habit of instant reaction.

P: Process

Your breath work creates the pause that then allows time, even if only for a few seconds, for rational processing to occur. When simply reacting, there is no pause and no room for rational thought to occur. Reaction is pure impulse. <u>Your job is to realize your ego's involvement and shift it around.</u> This may take the form of catching your automatic judgments about the person or situation and shifting your negative thoughts to positive. It could also be remembering your specific peace practice or the mantra you're using that day. Or, it could even be breaking habits of addiction by remembering: **all satisfaction is temporary** and that _____ (fill in the blank with your addiction of choice) **won't bring you lasting peace or happiness**. Whatever impulsive behavior may be trying to escape you, take some time to find and process rational thought instead of getting lost in the delusion your ego would have you perceive instead of reality.

Always remember: There is never a reason good enough to be out of alignment with peace.

I've worked with couples who yell at their children and spouse. They justify this by saying that the children wouldn't listen otherwise, or the spouse needed the escalation in volume before they'd take what was said seriously. However, this approach is the easy — and even lazy — way of communication since it's easier to "shut things down quick" or motivate everyone into action out of fear and aggression than it is to cultivate calm yet strong pathways of communication, inspiration, and cooperation. If you observe teachers in a classroom or parents with kids in public, you'll find that the ones who yell have the least control. Not because their children are worse than others — but because the parent (or teacher) lacks strong self-awareness and self-control, thus can't properly lead anyone else.

For PPR to work effectively, it's important that we adopt peace as our true north, taking to heart the teaching that there truly is *never a reason good enough to act out of alignment with peace.* If we don't believe that sentence, then we will continue to react because we subconsciously believe it's the best course of action to get the results we want.

R: Respond

The final step in this acronym is "R" for "Response". Choosing to respond to life's difficulties rather than react to them is potentially the number one, ultimate transforming factor in creating a life of inner peace. Why? Because if we never learn to respond and continue to react forevermore, nothing will change. Our "bad" habits will remain, our addictions, relationship conflicts, negative ongoing emotions of suffering… all of these will remain! Why? Because it's all us — no one else. Once we drop the blame game, our lives begin to transform because we start changing the ways in which we communicate and respond to life.

The way we respond to life is the way life will respond to us.

In everyday life and in regular conversations, Response is simply the practice of not being judgmental, unkind, harsh, or over-analyzing and over-assuming in our interactions. When we feel triggered or have the impulse to say something in reaction, we take the time to slow down and process the situation before we speak. We may even ask some questions for further clarity before we give an answer or our opinion. (Awesome practice there!). As we learn to mindfully respond, we become gentle and curious in our speech, rather than hard and opinionated. The same goes for our inner thoughts, not just our outer words.

There are a few more meanings that we give to the letter "R" in the PPR equation.

PP_R_: R=Release

The longer we do this work, the more we'll notice that we don't automatically form opinions about things, that we naturally begin to be more accepting and understanding. Thus, the Response may never come, and we gracefully Release what our mind chewed on for a brief instant.

PP_R_: R=Retreat (Reflect and Return)

For those of us just starting out in this practice, we may sometimes become too emotionally charged and heated during a triggering moment to Respond or Release right away. If we tried, our response would still come out hard and opinionated! (And we sure aren't ready to Release it!) So, the practice changes to Retreat. We withdraw for a short while to cool down and Reflect before Responding.

It is of extreme importance when we do leave a situation or conversation that we *disclaim up front* we are simply taking time to reflect and will be back to finish the conversation soon. Disclaiming is an act of mindfulness, respect, and kindness. Leaving without a word only causes further harm. Some people do this to avoid uncomfortable conversations that they often don't return to deal with — sweeping things under the rug until the next explosion.

Retreating must always be followed up with Returning when using the practice of PPR.

Some of us are escape artists and avoidists, who may misuse this Retreat version of PPR. Please always remember that you must still Respond to finish any and all difficult conversations. Leaving things unresolved only leads to further suffering down the road.

Concluding Thoughts

Each of these three steps may only take a few seconds when we're in the middle of a triggering experience, yet we must not let the simplicity or shortness of this exercise keep us from realizing its enormous power.

We tend to think our problems must have lengthy and complex solutions, when in reality, if we begin making small, every day and every moment changes to our lives — transformation occurs much more quickly. We may go on a retreat or visit a therapist and have a groundbreaking experience, but unless we begin making these subtle changes to our lives daily, that amazing high we experienced will eventually be replaced with the daily struggles we experienced before.

PPR changes the way we respond to life, which in turn begins to transform the life around us — because *we* have transformed!

≫ ≫ ≫ ≪ ≪ ≪

Now, with the wisdom from Mastery of Thought & Impulse under our belts, it's time to expand our awareness even further into understanding and mastering emotion.

Tenet Three:

Mastery of Emotion

Flashback:

One of the greatest (and hardest) lessons I learned was from my first love experience, which brought out all my co-dependent attachments and insecurities.

I was in college to become a minister, and he was signed up for Marine boot camp. Our love was dynamic to say the least, since he and I both had strong characters and personalities. We challenged one another and seemed to bring out both the worst and the best in each other. Before meeting him, I never fully trusted anyone other than my parents, and he opened me up to the world of being someone's partner and sharing a life, rather than living solely for myself. I supported his dream to become a Marine, yet when he left, I made the decision to end the relationship, which I regretted for a full four years thereafter. On a soul level, I felt it was the right thing to do, yet my heart wept many tears of sorrow each night.

For two years, I sank back into depression and was unable to live in the present moment since, in my thoughts, I kept reliving our time together. My belief system was that our love was the kind found only "once in a lifetime", and because I was (and am) such an eccentric individual, he may very well have been the only one for me. It certainly seemed that way for four years, even as I met and dated plenty of other men.

Every time I went on a date, I felt like I was cheating on him, even after a year had passed. I vividly remember the first time I spent the night another man after him. Afterward, I went to the bathroom, looked in the mirror and began to cry. I eventually spiraled into randomly dating anyone who asked in my misguided attempts to fill the void in my heart. On one such date, I remember thinking, "How did I get here? I used to date such respectful men and here this guy is drunk, asleep on the couch and I'm lying on the floor trying to sleep with tears in my eyes, hugging his cat."

I had no control over my emotional state of being, and that was when

I decided enough was enough. It was time for me to let my old love go, release all illusions and stop reliving the past and/or living in hopes of a future with him. Neither existed in the here and now, and I had already wasted a few years of my life suffering for no reason other than my own inability to let things go. I had once again given my power away and it was time to reclaim it! I vowed never again to give my power away to another person by making my happiness dependent upon them. It was time to take responsibility for my own happiness.

*The person I am today, a decade later, would have responded to my first love experience with pure acceptance. Because of our conflicting life paths, we had many conflicts in our budding relationship. Instead of being fully supportive, I allowed my attachment to him and my feelings of desire to cloud my peace and kindness. What I thought was love was actually the behaviors and mentality of ego on my part. Although love **was** present at the core, genuine love would not have eroded into the self-destructive behavior I displayed. This is why the teaching of un-attachment is so critical. Had I been in my peace, I would have still ended the relationship (because it was the most rational choice given that we were so young and on very different life paths). However, I would have done so from a genuine place of love — which would have shown itself as unconditional happiness for him and unconditional peace for me. The result? No karmic patterns of grief, living in the past, or participating in numerous unhealthy relationships in the future.*

Peace becomes possible when we cease to let our emotions be swayed by the conditions in the outside world. When we are on autopilot and unaware of our ability to take control, life is a rollercoaster of emotions: up and down, left and right, and all around depending on the rails of external conditions. The so-called negative situations in our lives cause us to feel depressed, angry, and stressed. And to counteract them, we often wait for a happy occurrence to shift our moods, or we chase happiness, planning ahead for our joy or relief. The game we play when we give our emotional power away to other things or other people is a dangerous one. The goal is to be at peace here in the now, not waiting for all tracks in our life to line up just right before we can feel at peace and be happy. *Peace is not something to chase – it is something to be. Our mission is to embody and become peace.*

A student of mine once pointed out that the wording of the mantra we use forces us to acknowledge that we are the peace and that peace is not dependent on any external factor:

"'I Am Peace.' I've meditated a lot on the phrase you gave us last week. It seems to have a very different connotation than 'I am at peace', or 'I am peaceful', or even 'I feel at peace'. I have tried substituting words for 'peace' like 'I am happy', 'I am human', or 'I am love'. It appears that you are teaching me that Peace is a state of being that is not conditional upon other people's situations, or the environment. This is not an easy thing that you are asking of me, Reverend!" – Ric W.

The reason I work with peace is because it is the foundation upon which all other uplifting emotions can be built. Without peace, all good vibes can easily be washed away when a single external force upsets us and causes us to lose our balance. Without that foundation, our moods are leaves easily blown away on the wind.

Each mastery layers upon the next. Without awareness of our thoughts and the ability to control our impulses, we will never be able to master our emotions. Our emotions are slaves to our impulses, and our impulses are slaves to our thoughts. If we can catch our thoughts, impulses, and emotions before they turn into the actions that cause a snowball effect of drama, stress, and pain, then we can shift the course of emotional discord. An impulse of frustration generally leads to anger, just as spontaneous laughter and random acts of kindness turn into happiness.

The way I look at it is: some emotions cause lingering effects that take longer to shift. And if we can catch their precursors before they turn into the lingering versions, we can take control! For example, we can catch and shift feelings of disempowerment before they turn into depression. The same applies to the other end of the spectrum. Positive affirmations and intentional gratitude activities work well to uplift our moods. An ounce of gratitude now can turn into a pound of joy later. When we develop a greater sense of awareness, we unlock the ability to make conscious choices when these situations arise. For example, I'm not without frustrations — they do occasionally arise, yet they rarely last more than a couple of minutes (often only a few seconds) before I shift and transmute them into something more beneficial. It all goes back to our thoughts.

≫ ≫ ≫ ≪ ≪ ≪

Everyone is doing the best they can with what they know, and we are
all here to learn and grow.

Yes, everyone is doing the best they can with what they know, and we are all here to learn and grow. (That statement deserved an encore.) Actually, let's repeat it again: **Everyone is doing the best they can with what they know, and we are all here to learn and grow.** What a freeing thought! I invite you to write it down and revisit it daily, for if you implant this thought into your belief system, you will surely notice a happier shift in your perception of the world. For starters, when you hold this thought, forgiveness of self and others becomes easier. And it is often lack of forgiveness that blocks individuals from achieving mastery of emotion.

Not forgiving ourselves and holding onto guilt and regret, or not forgiving others and holding onto bitterness and resentment won't benefit us, or the world. All unforgiveness lowers our vibration and acts as fuel for the machines of war. (WAR: We. Are. Right.) Release the need to be right! Realize that every war begins with separation of hearts in the home where these angry, fearful emotions first take root.

Therefore, what gets passed on from generation to generation are not only physical global problems, but also energetic blocks, since whatever we do not resolve within ourselves in our lifetime is left to the next generation to resolve. We can see this in ancestry lines and in karmic patterns. This "energetic baggage" we pass on to our families also applies to groups of collective consciousnesses and the planet as a whole. Thus, forgiveness is not just some fancy ideal; it is a **must** if we are ever to move forward toward a more peaceful planet as homo-luminous beings.

If we remove the duality involved, meaning we remove the rights and wrongs, and we focus on the heart — we realize that feeling at peace with each other always takes priority. Feeling GOOD is what matters. Holding onto bitterness is like being stabbed by a thorn and keeping it embedded in your skin so you can show others how much you have suffered. Take it out! Release it! Let it go! Live in the present moment! You were pricked once, and every day since then, you've allowed the wound to fester.

People who suffer the most often inflict the most pain onto others. Compassion for them can be found through understanding this. When someone is suffering internally, often the only reality they can see is one of pain, and their only knowledge is how to be a victim or an abuser. That's all they're able to communicate because it truly is "the best they know". So, holding on to the thorn of resentment doesn't help them or you, but fostering compassion and forgiveness will.

Did you know that forgiveness is only necessary for

people who get upset? And the only people who get upset are those who do not accept reality as it is in the present moment. When we live in the present moment, each pain, each hurt is released, quickly becoming the past that we no longer live in. The upset and easily frustrated individual will focus on and be stuck at, "Why did you do that?!" while the individual at peace has already moved forward to the fresh next moment.

I cannot tell you personally how many times people have apologized to me when I have no idea what they're talking about! "I'm sorry I did that," they tell me. And my response to them is, "Did what?" or, "That was so long ago — I haven't called it to memory in years!"

For people who struggle mightily with forgiveness, I invite you to try accepting the past as the past. Oftentimes, people feel they need to forgive before they can be present, yet it works the other way around. If we accept reality as it is now, the need to forgive vanishes by default. We only need forgive those whom we harbor ill will towards. If we remove the ill will by living totally in the now, it releases our involvement with them in the present moment.

Forgiveness of self is also something that we grapple with. The same rule of thumb applies. Accept the past as the past and realize that each morning, you become a new person who doesn't need to carry old baggage into the new day with you. It's amazing how many people ruin the beauty of today with the sorrows of yesterday. Yesterday doesn't exist anymore! If ever I feel foolish or guilty about something I've done, I learn from it and attempt to do better the next time. Shame or guilt serves no one. Such feelings actually keep us down, often lowering the vibrations of those around us, too. **Living in the present moment is the recurring baptism of the soul, forever purifying each new day with a new you.**

Embracing the present moment brings us closer to emotional mastery. And through mastering present moment awareness, eventually we reach a place of un-attachment.

Un-attachment (as opposed to detachment) is the acceptance that each and every person is responsible for his or her own reality, and that our joy, peace, security, and sense of love is not dependent on any other person or situation. We each are responsible for our own emotional wellbeing. Let me repeat that since it's worth repeating: **We are each responsible for our own emotional wellbeing!** No one can make us feel anything unless we have agreed to it somewhere in our conscious or subconscious minds. Emotions do not arise from a situation unless there is a deep-seated belief attached to the occurrence that gives it a negative or positive meaning.

*Note: The difference between detachment and un-attachment from my point of view: **Detachment** is apathy or aloofness toward other people. **Un-attachment** acknowledges and honors other people while choosing not to let them influence your emotional wellbeing. Detached means "I don't care", while un-attached means "I care, although I'm not going to alter my emotional state because of your emotions, words, or actions."*

As we practice and hone our un-attachment, we begin to see the world as a "playground of growth" where our souls come to interact with each other in physical form so that we may learn lessons and expand our consciousness. We begin to honor each individual soul's journey more and more and grow less and less attached to the duality involved in assigning "rights" and "wrongs" to everyone else's choices. Un-attachment means allowing other people to live their lives however they choose, without placing judgments, developing opinions, or giving them our "two cents' worth". If they ask, certainly we can give them our views; however, it is still none of our business to analyze or criticize how they live their lives.

If we find ourselves focusing too much on others' lives, chances are we're ignoring our own issues. As I'm fond of saying, "It's best not to gripe about your neighbor's weedy yard when your house paint is chipping off." The deeper meaning behind this is that when we stick our noses into other people's lives with a judgmental mindset, it lowers our vibration. And when we become overly attached to other people, drama often ensues.

Freedom is a fabulous thing. When we allow people to come in and out of our lives as they choose, it not only promotes peace; it often makes our relationships with them stronger. This promotes a beautiful ebb and flow, since we desire the same loving treatment from others. After all, each of our lives involves perpetual growth, thus we must ensure we are giving everyone the opportunity to grow and become someone new in our eyes, rather than holding onto the person they used to be or who we want them to be.

However, sometimes we really care about people, so we get attached to their growing pains. When this occurs, it is very important to understand that pity and over-empathizing helps no one. For one, it makes *you* feel unwell; and two, it doesn't help them get better. What helps is when you, as the observer, do not get attached and lower your vibration due to their struggles. Through un-attachment, you maintain a state of peace and become a beaming example of unconditional peace, sharing your radiant glow with them and all others throughout the world.

Additional Notes

Not being fully present is the root cause of most issues—it leads to miscommunication, exhaustion, and distancing ourselves from the hearts of the people we love.

Living in the present moment allows us to embrace all life has to offer as we become fully aware of our thoughts and actions. When our thoughts pull us out of the present moment and our attention becomes divided, everything we experience in the present becomes divided. Being fully present allows us to receive the full joy of sharing company with someone. Being fully present allows us to do our work well, and not have to take it home with us at the end of the day. Being fully present allows us to share in the joys of home life, and if the home life gets "out of sorts", being present allows us to clear up the dysfunction. Being present allows us to creatively express ourselves. Being present allows us to unwind when the day is done, rest easy, recharge and be energized and ready to embrace the following day.

Practice 3
Emotional Wave Surfing
(*Mastery of Emotion*)

As we have learned through the Three Masteries, all thoughts and emotions are temporary. Fleeting though they may be, these feelings can still sometimes overwhelm us like a tsunami crashing down on and all around us. These "emotional waves" vary in strength and come and go incessantly, just as the waves in the ocean do, and that's why we must learn to vibrationally "surf" them.

The next time you find yourself becoming swallowed up in a negative thought pattern, an impulsive urge, or you are already trapped in a heavy emotion—stop and pause as you learned in *Practice Two: PPR*. Process the situation, and with all your might, pull yourself into the awareness that what is presently occurring in your mind and body is a temporary sensation based on a temporary situation.

Begin using *Practice One: The File Exchange* to sort through your thoughts, replacing negative ones with positive (or neutral) ones. Recognize that the impulse or reaction your ego encourages as a solution won't bring lasting relief or satisfaction. And most important, honor that whatever emotion you are feeling isn't something to judge or resist, it is simply the natural byproduct of your egoic attachment to the situation and your subconscious insecurities or fears manifesting as false reality.

False reality: Incomplete or biased perception, usually controlled by egoic fear, that triggers an emotional overreaction.

The *half-truth* and the *true-Truth* of reality: All experiences and realities are true to some extent (half-truths), because we make them so in our minds. Thus, they have a very real, physical effect on our minds and bodies, altering our life choices. Yet, the true-Truth (or, as I like to say, the true-True) is seen when we remove all opinion, all mental and emotional bias from a situation, and observe what occurs factually without getting involved in duality. Although we may never reach perfection in this — since it's impossible to know every aspect of every situation — we will certainly gain much more clarity, which in turn will allow us to pierce the veils of our delusions, no matter how painful a situation may be.

Remember: There is never a reason good enough to speak or act out of alignment with peace.

The practice of emotional wave surfing, at its heart, involves activating our peaceful logic and reason so we may remain un-attached (not detached, mind you) during all conflicting situations. This allows us to make the healthiest decisions possible. When we become emotionally swallowed up by tragedy, it is of our own doing — not the tragedy's. Being consumed by grief, guilt, shame, fear, or anger helps absolutely no one, nor does feeling pity or itching for retribution. In our everyday lives, we must practice "surfing" above our emotions, so we don't react with or "become" those emotions, thus losing our strength, will, and the ability to effectively communicate and act free of bias.

PPR curbs the tide; The File Exchange transmutes (changes) it, and Emotional Wave Surfing allows us to intentionally direct the flow, and our flow, of energy.

Exploring Emotional Ebbs and Flows

Even the most astute students of self-mastery techniques

will occasionally find themselves in the thrall of heavy emotion. This heaviness on the heart or mind may last a day, a week, or even a month. All of this is perfectly okay and even normal, due to the nature of human life. The beauty of Emotional Wave Surfing is that we can recognize our emotional heaviness, yet never act on it, or react because of it. The heaviness morphs into a manageable "companion" next to us that doesn't interfere with our work, relationships, or our ability to be present. Fighting or denying its existence makes it much worse, yet if we simply acknowledge it and carry on with our everyday lives — it becomes quite tolerable and even non-interruptive.

I sometimes share a controversial approach to suicidal thoughts: They are okay to have, "okay" meaning there need not be any judgment involving them. Some may argue this as dangerous to teach and support, yet I've seen evidence, time and time again, that it is **believing** *that we are "wrong" or "bad", or that the thoughts we are having are "wrong" or "bad", that further escalates suicidal tendencies. What if we simply acknowledged their existence and said to the part of ourselves that thinks them, "Hello. I see you hiding over there, and it's okay to feel the way you do. When you're ready to share* **why** *you feel like extinguishing your life, I'm here to listen." No judgment, no force — just acceptance, kindness, and compassion towards the self. The result of this self-love is that the suicidal thoughts fade away, either on their own, or through epiphanies the individual has by becoming open and receptive rather than fearful and combative.*

The beauty of this collective work, and specifically this third practice, is that the more we respond with patience, kindness, and compassion towards our ever-fluctuating emotions, they grow less severe over time. When we are calm and collected, even during the most painful situations, we aren't "stirring the fire", so more sparks fly causing wounds we must attend to later. When we react, we are "burning" ourselves again on top of the original "burn" received. This is why so many people suffer from perpetual emotional pain.

Furthering Your Practice

If you would like a more tangible practice for Emotional Wave Surfing, make a T-chart of the half-truths and true-Truths of your situation. Writing these down will help you discern and decipher what is going on inside so you can more effectively respond and surf the "emotional wave" you're currently experiencing.

Additionally, a helpful mantra to memorize and repeat is: *"I recognize the impermanence of this feeling and emotion."*

Remembering the wisdom of impermanence — that nothing last forever — is an excellent tool to use when traversing the ups and downs of our emotional terrain.

Concluding Thoughts

Refrain from ever making statements such as, "I **am** sad" or "I **am** angry". You are NOT these emotions, thus changing these expressions to "I feel sadness" or "I feel anger" is much more fluid and honors the temporariness of the emotion. When we claim negative emotions with an "I **am**" statement, those emotions get programmed into our subconscious mind, making them more and more consistent aspects of our personalities that we must recondition later using *The File Exchange* practice learned in *Mastery of Thought*.

On a rare occasion, a dream takes me back to a sad place, and I awaken with a funk that lingers throughout the day. It is akin to the depression I once felt, no rhyme or reason to it, just a persistent numb, disempowered sadness. On these rare days, I express to my husband by saying, "Today, I'm feeling a touch of depression, yet

I'm aware it won't last long." And sure enough, the spell fades throughout the day and is completely gone by the next morning.

In the past, I might have tried to analyze the emotional wave rather than surf it, which only ever gave it more power to consume me. Now, I am able to still be fully productive in whatever I am working on and remain fully present in my relationships, while surfing through the feelings and emotions that are quite brief because I allow them to ebb and flow, in and out, without resistance.

Part Two:
The Three Illusions

The Vibrational Aura

The energy of our thoughts, words, actions, and emotions collectively create the frequency of our vibrational aura.

Disclaimer:

Although the vibrational aura is generally thought of as more in the realm of spirituality and metaphysics, if you find yourself a skeptic as to its physical reality, think back to a time when you felt energy from someone or something. As you read this chapter, consider the vibrational aura to be an explanation for statements such as, "The energy was so thick in the room I could cut it with a knife!" and "Her positive vibe was contagious, and I couldn't help but feel good when I spent the day with her."

Whether you take the following information literally or metaphorically, something we can all agree on (even science is finding proof) is that there is indeed an energy emitted by the combination of our thoughts, emotions, words, and actions, and we can feel its effect.

*Note: Now is an excellent time to define **alignment**, a word used throughout this book. **Alignment** means being in harmony with one's mind, body, heart, and spirit – thus creating an inner peace and outer calm. **Vibrational alignment** is very similar, adding the harmony of one's thoughts, words, actions, and emotions to create unity versus non-alignment, which leads to the creation of ignorance, chaos, and duality.*

≫ ≫ ≫ ≪ ≪ ≪

Imagine for a moment that everyone could see auras as clear as we see day, that each of us has an energetic field around us that can be perceived. Depending on their color and flow, our auras showcase the vibrations we emanate into the world, as well as what we attract and manifest into our own lives.

Want to know the fun, crazy, and wild part? We may not be able to see them, yet these vibrational auras are real and influence our lives at all times. Some people do have the gift of the ability to see them. I do not, though I can sense them and feel their pull on myself and others. This understanding led me to the insight that I now share.

Whenever we focus on the problems and stresses of our lives — get frustrated by personal, communal, or even global issues — we lower our vibration, which causes our auras to become tainted with Dis-Ease. Anytime we are angry, envious, or judgmental, we become walking toxic energy, our vibrationally auras polluting the air around us.

It's humorous for me to imagine people engaged in drama and stress suddenly becoming aware of the noxious vapors they are releasing. If people could see, or *smell*, these fumes — they'd never allow their vibrations to dip so severely in public again! I invite you to use this vibrational imagery as a mindful practice; to really think about what your energy morphs into, and exudes, as you experience different moods.

Remember, when we are upset, bitter, or stressed, our auras become clouded and stagnant, oozing out like a cold, black lagoon. If these negative emotions are allowed to flourish, they may even become toxic, bringing illness to all those who come within range of them.

When we are at peace and share in gratitude, our auras shine bright and flow warmly outward to uplift everyone who comes into contact with them. Additionally, our vibrational auras automatically adjust our frequency to attract and manifest into our lives even more of what we give out. "Like energy" always attracts "like energy" exponentially.

Our thoughts, emotions, words, and actions each carry separate vibrations that make up the collective vibration of our auras. These vibrational auras are what the Law of Attraction works upon and the Universe adheres to. Whatever our vibrations are, those are the kinds of experiences we will attract into our lives.

When it comes to mastering the Law of Attraction, it's not as simple as just thinking positive thoughts. Our emotions, words, and actions — which have their roots in our beliefs — must also be in alignment. We will touch more on all of this later; for now, let's focus on the power of thought and vibration.

Imagine that there is a laser beam that shoots out of your third-eye, the area in the center of your forehead just above your physical eyes. Now, imagine that whatever you put your mental focus on swiftly multiplies and magnifies because the laser beam shoots forth a growth formula that increases the emotions involved while also attracting more like energy to it. For better or worse, this is what happens every time we think of a situation that triggers an emotion within us.

If we truly take a vulnerable look at our entire life, we find that it is always a 100% reflection of our inner beliefs — the ways in which we perceive and judge the world. What we focus on, we get more of…every single time. And the full measure of what we believe we deserve and what we're worth is exactly what we're given. Our mental constructs about the reality of life forever and always manifest as the blessings and curses we experience in our physical reality.

How ironic it is then, to realize how many of us are masochists! That even if we found ourselves in paradise, the majority of us would, by choice, focus on everything outside the present moment and cause ourselves suffering by thinking about Dis-Ease! Too many of us would dwell on a past that no longer exists instead of realizing that everything in the present moment is wonderful. What great paradoxes we humans are capable of!

We create reality from our thoughts *about* reality, which are infinite in their variations. In order to perceive and create a brighter reality, we first must be a vibrational match for it, since, as mentioned above, we could be surrounded by beauty and peace in a paradise, yet still feel unworthy of it and suffer because of our thoughts. This is precisely why global peace doesn't exist. People are so intent on fixing and healing everyone else in the world rather than focusing on coming into personal vibrational harmony and healing themselves.

We each create our own "heaven" or "hell" every waking moment of our lives. This is why mystics throughout history have always placed emphasis on the importance of the present moment. It is all that ever exists.

And our present moment vibration is the reality that we will see and experience. We can only perceive what we vibrate. Conversely; we cannot perceive what we do not vibrate. Using a dualistic analogy, an angel will always find the redeeming quality in a demon, and a demon will always find sin in an angel. This is not because of what they are; it's because of the vibration they send forth and how it colors their vision of reality. It's the same with us mere mortals' mental overlay.

Only peace will bring peace. This is why going to war for peace doesn't work. Peace and war are not vibrational matches and cannot co-exist. Trying to fix anything by embracing any part of it is the equivalent of having sexual intercourse to become celibate. It just doesn't work that way! If we want peace, we must be peace. If we want respect and trust, we must first be trustworthy and respectful while actively giving trust and respect to others. It all comes back to our vibrational auras! What are we embodying and emitting out into the Universe? We can't wait for something outside ourselves to change; we must actively *be* the change if we wish to see the result.

As we step into the Three Illusions, our firm grasp on the role our vibrational energy plays in our life will help us dive deeper into the layers of wisdom regarding the nature of ignorance, chaos, and duality.

Tenet Four:

Ignorance is an Illusion; We Seek Understanding

Flashback:

A lesson I learned the hard way: Never let your desire to have an accepting heart towards others keep you from establishing strong boundaries. The hurricane may come blasting at our door, yet we don't have to open up and invite it in. It's important to recognize the difference between a hurricane – a powerful, damaging storm – and a light spring shower.

A married couple once joined our community for a few months, and boy howdy, were they a rambunctious duo! They waved many red flags; however, because I had vowed to be accepting of and inviting to everyone, I was blinded by my own wishful thinking.

When attending their first sermon, one of the first things the couple said was that someone in the room was making them feel incredibly uncomfortable and this person had "bad energy". They came into the community with a dualistic mindset, found someone to project that mindset onto, and began to create separation against a person they hadn't even met. From that moment on, they pointed fingers, felt attacked by others, gossiped and formed cliques, and, near the end of their sojourn with us, they also slandered my name. To say the least, dealing with this was exhausting – and all of it was due to illusion on their part! The only so-called "bad energy" that existed was what they brought into the space, and, when they eventually left the community, the negativity went with them.

Their reality was colored by their vibration and belief systems. In other words, the experiences they had with other people was dictated by the energy they brought with them wherever they went. And, as we learned in the previous chapter, their energy also affected everyone around them.

The irony was that all the red flags they waved were there from day one. The lesson learned was that when people show who they are from the start, believe them and accept it! Expecting them to change, or thinking you can change them, isn't accepting them, even though you may have good intentions.

We can confuse being accepting with being a doormat for some people to wipe their muddy feet on. I was so concerned with making them feel secure and welcome that I forgot to use discernment and set clear boundaries. To this day, I accept that couple for who they are. I think they are marvelous souls doing what they came here to do in this life – learn and grow like the rest of us. They had many beautiful qualities about them that I did see and appreciate. However, that doesn't mean I will now invite them in when I'm aware they (the hurricane) may abuse and cause further destruction to me, my home and my family.

I did (and do) understand and have compassion for the reasons behind their abuse. I did my best to offer assistance. For now, I leave their whirlwind of agitation out in the open field where it has plenty of room to blow out its anger. If and when the storm subsides, then the opportunity to extend an invitation may be revisited.

≫ ≫ ≫ ≪ ≪ ≪

Ignorance is an illusion; we seek understanding. Compassion paves the way to understanding and understanding paves the way to acceptance.

I teach my students to think beyond duality, opinions, and taking sides. We must always be open and willing to shift our perceptions. The moment we attach ourselves to an opinion or belief about something, we limit ourselves, closing doors to all other possibilities.

This closing of doors is what I call ignorance. Ignorance is often simply defined as "not knowing"; however, as used herein, it is a willful state – the choice to close our hearts and minds to the greater freedom of possibility. If we constantly keep ourselves open, then the shackles of ignorance will never restrain us.

What is asked of us is to walk through life with an agnostic mind—accepting our limited perception with humbleness, never forming opinions on what's unknown. And as for what is "known", we must always be willing to change our opinion when new information presents itself. Nothing is ever set in stone. We vow to seek understanding in all areas of life, including those areas that make us uncomfortable.

Never close the door of your heart to anyone. They may not be in vibrational alignment today, so you must place distance between your physical self and them for your own wellbeing, but later in life, they may awaken and seek your forgiveness, understanding, and peace. If you close the door to your heart, when they do return, they will find their way blocked and may walk away without even knocking, since it took all their courage just to approach the door. However, if you leave the door to your warm heart open and they see your welcoming energy, a beautiful healing and consciousness-expanding experience is likely to follow. If they never return that's okay, too, since everyone is on their own beautiful path. It's never our place to judge the choices and/or outcome of anyone's journey.

On the path toward peace we always seek understanding, even when—in situations that appear black and white—there seems to be none. Truly, that is never the case; there are always layers upon layers of understanding, and it's our responsibility to peel away the layers until we reach the one that illuminates before making a decision that could alter other lives.

Compassion is the key to keeping our hearts and minds open. Compassion dissolves ignorance. Let me repeat that: **Compassion dissolves ignorance**. Also, as reminders, **people are always doing the best they can with what they know,** and **people who suffer the most inflict the most pain**. These two beliefs allow us to transcend the duality of taking sides.

When I was in sixth grade and experiencing the worst of the bullying abuse, my mom asked me if I felt any anger towards the bullies. My answer was "no". I shared with her that I understood them. I understood that they did not truly know what they were doing and that they were in pain. I said I was aware that their own pain blinded them so all they knew was to treat others as they were being treated. I had compassion. Then Mom asked me if I forgave them. My answer was that there was nothing to forgive.

Though I was unaware of it at the time, I was the embodiment of this tenet. I chose understanding over ignorance. If I had become angry over my mistreatment, my own vision would have been blinded and all channels of further understanding and compassion would have been closed. Chaos reigned around me, yet peace remained in the core of my heart.

≫ ≫ ≫ ≪ ≪ ≪

Acceptance is the second key to keeping our hearts and minds open. As mentioned in my personal story at the beginning of this chapter, acceptance does not mean being someone's doormat. Acceptance is respectfully acknowledging others as they are, at whatever stage they have reached in their lives in this moment, and not projecting our opinions onto them — whether these opinions are "negative" judgments of contrast or "positive" judgments that lead us to want to help them or "fix" them.

It is absolutely necessary to adopt the belief of "live and let live" where our fellow human beings are concerned. The beliefs "I know best" or "I know better" are incredibly dangerous and ignorant since not a single person alive "knows" what is best for any other person alive. Remember, we are spiritual beings living a physical experience, and as such we may think we see the whole picture, yet on a spiritual level each soul is working out their own karmic patterns in a portrait that is as vast as the Universe. "Saving" people from their pain can be quite ignorant because, in trying to rescue them, we may actually be keeping them from the karmic lessons they signed up to learn. We are merely asked to be guides, not saviors. When we get into savior mode, we are actually acting from our egos.

Furthermore, when we ourselves are not truly in a place of peace, yet we go out and try to create peace in the world, what we actually make is a fragmented and sometimes even corrupt form of peace. This happens because only peace can create peace, and unless we are the embodiment of it, we are projecting our bias of what peace should look like onto other people.

Being at peace manifests as accepting reality as it is and people as they are. Embodying peace is, in fact, the very essence of what it means to experience freedom, which then allows us to offer this same freedom (through acceptance) to others.

Some have the confused idea that peace can only occur when all the colors on a palette are the same. The actuality of peace is accepting each color's differences and seeing the beauty each possesses. Peace is the freedom that comes from individuality and the co-creativity that arises from cooperation. When you are red and at peace, you can appreciate blue and not need it to become red like you. And vice-versa. The color not at peace wants all the colors to be like it, so that it can experience peace. Black and white photos have a beauty of their own, yet the world as a whole is one filled with other colors. And in order to paint a complete portrait of the world, it's necessary to use every color in existence. It's time we accept all the colors, even the ones that are not the same as we are – or not what we'd choose to use to create our own individual portrait.

When people of differing religions or countries harm others to create peace, it's out of the compulsion to make all colors the same. It's why they also think war is necessary to "keep peace". They believe they must force others into submission before others force them into submission. Those who don't possess inner peace only know war, only know how to throw hand grenades at a situation. The grenades detonate as they project their fragmented concepts of peace out onto the world, scattering shards of delusion like shrapnel, perpetuating pain and anger.

Once we can accept reality as it is and don't need to change it, we can begin to take steps toward creating a brighter reality for ourselves and others, coming from a place of understanding. But when we are motivated to change reality due to our discomfort with it, we aren't thinking clearly.

Extreme suffering exists in the world because too many of us spend most of our time judging everyone and everything, and through these judgments, we perpetuate suffering. People are so focused on changing outside conditions, ignoring the judgment and separation in their own hearts. It is the kind of ignorance that creates illusion; thus, we must always seek understanding.

Judgment is contrary to the vibration of unconditional love. Judgment and love do not exist in the same place at the same time, just as war and peace cannot co-exist in the same place at the same time. Bringing ourselves into vibrational alignment with peace and love will shift the vibrations first in our homes and then echo outward into our communities. Our communities will then reach out to the rest of the state and country, and the country will reach out to the world.

The last topic I want to touch on in this chapter is **vibrational expectation**, which is vibrationally attracting what we expect from life. Once we form an opinion about something or someone, we forever afterward receive experiences that are hued by our beliefs due to the Law of Attraction. The decisions we make in our minds become the underlying themes that manifest as the different directions we chose and, from them, the ultimate course that our lives take. The reality that we see around us is always a direct reflection of our beliefs about others, ourselves, and the world as a whole. Once we have a thought about something as true, it becomes our belief, and once it becomes our belief, it becomes set in our vibration—constantly sending out energy that attracts the same kind of energy to us in the situations that arise.

This means each experience we have will reinforce that particular belief within us and blind us to all other information coming in. Remember, just because we feel or see something doesn't automatically mean it's true! A simple shift in perception can drastically change what we see and feel about a situation.

As shared in the intro story, the couple's belief system about other people and themselves set in motion situation after situation that reinforced their "negative" reality. Someone forgot to respond to their email, and it became a personal insult. They overheard their name mentioned in a conversation, and it was assumed they were being "negatively" gossiped about. Someone wasn't as warm to them as they'd expected, so they thought that person was out to get them. In every experience, our beliefs hue situations as "negative" or "positive", and through the activation of the Law of Attraction, peace or drama is cultivated.

Our belief system becomes a filter. The more "set in stone" our dualistic beliefs and opinions are, the heavier and denser the filter is, and the thicker the filter is, the less co-creative information can enter. Just remember: as long as a "negative" belief exists within us, the world around us will continue to reinforce that belief as true, and it then becomes negative self-certainty. It's our job to recognize the illusion and take back control, shifting that thought to something more beneficial for our highest good. Something isn't "real" or "true" just because it has "always" been what we've believed and experienced. We make it real by believing in it and feeding it power. The same is accurate for, "just because we think a thought or feel a feeling doesn't necessarily make it a true thought or true feeling grounded in actual reality."

Our call to action is to always seek clarity and understanding in life, not make assumptions. We often jump to conclusions and emotionally feel Dis-Ease due to the projected illusions that form our distorted realities. When we live in the present moment and keep an open mind, always asking for clarity versus assuming the worst, peace is much more easily cultivated and maintained.

Practice 4
The Love Question
(Ignorance is an Illusion;
We Seek Understanding)

There are times in our lives when our ego doesn't want us to communicate, and yet, communicate we must. This is what walking the path of peace requires of us; otherwise, we'll fall back into unhealthy silence or reactive communication that ultimately leads to misunderstandings and emotional conflict.

How recurrently have you pulled away from people in your life because you felt upset, disrespected, unappreciated, or hurt? How frequently have you attempted to communicate these feelings, only to let your frustrated emotions spill out, promoting aggressiveness or defensiveness rather than a calm interaction with the other person? These slip-ups in communication happen much too often. Although there's no need to judge or criticize yourself for the miscommunications, there is a more peaceful way once you learn the associated teachings.

The practice:

"How can I love you better?"

The above question is a humbling one. My husband and I ask it of each other at least once per month. At this newlywed stage in our marriage the answer is often, "Nothing at the moment – I feel happy and satisfied but thank you for asking", yet there have been various times when one of us felt slightly "off" and requested deeper understanding and support from the other. Early in our budding relationship we developed strong roots, so we were still able to communicate when those roots hit rocky ground. It became second nature to share any and all thoughts, feelings, and emotions with each other. The result: Slight worries or frustrations never become major emotions like resentment, fear, or anger. By tending to the foundational soil of our relationship, our love was able to grow unencumbered.

In many relationships this isn't the case because new couples ignore establishing a healthy foundation of communication and respect in favor of the excitement and passion of the new relationship. They focus solely on their attachment to each other and move in together too soon because their roots are too shallow. It's no surprise to anyone when their love falls over like a weak sapling the first time a storm hits.

Today, after you read this chapter and practice section, ask someone in your life how you can love them better. This person may be your significant other, a parent, child, friend, or even your boss, or fellow employees or colleagues. In the workplace you may change the wording to some variation of "What can I do to help you feel more heard and appreciated?" Love, after all, is a word that carries many meanings, which, when broken down, greatly help us to understand why we must cultivate it everywhere we go and in every connection we have.

Love as a verb (Love in action): kindness, respect, appreciation, honesty, compassion, listening, understanding, accepting, sharing happiness, being joyful and peaceful. **Love as a noun:** laughter, dignity, grace, and unattachment (freedom)**...and SO much more!**

It's important to point out that love is NOT lust nor desire — since both create further attachment, craving, and frustration, whether they are satisfied or not. A power struggle often ensues between the pursuer and the pursued, the giver and the receiver.

If peace is not in the heart—it is not love, it is ego. If your relationship doesn't promote the above "positive" (unifying) definitions of love—it is not love in action. Love may still be present, especially in parent-child relationships, but it is clouded by the "negative" (separating) emotions of ego.

Asking the people in our lives, "How can I love you better?" humbles us and circumvents our ego. This practice removes our ignorant roadblocks and builds a direct pathway of communication and understanding between two people. Remember: compassion dissolves ignorance. And when we truly and fully hear other people, we can't help but learn and better understand their pain. The only way our anger, resentments, and strong desires of separation or fighting can persist is by ignoring the other person's perspective. If we are willfully blind to another's viewpoint, we see only our self-reinforcing opinions and trap ourselves in self-fulfilling prophesies of pain and patterns of unhappiness and broken relationships.

The next time you find someone in extreme pain and anger, even if it's directed at you—ask them how you can love them better. Or, if they're someone you don't know too well, ask them some version of this question. When people are in pain and emotional distress it's because they're trapped in a reality of separation. Asking pierces the veil of delusion and creates immediate action steps that provide a great deal of insight. Just don't be surprised if the person you ask can't answer you. It may be the first time they were ever asked this question!

When you're feeling like you're not being heard or seen, ask this love question of yourself. Ask yourself how you can love yourself better—or imagine someone asking you the question. The answers you'll find can then be shared with the people in your life, so they can better understand how to love you if they haven't learned this teaching themselves. Please also remember: Never expect anyone to automatically know how to love you if you haven't communicated clearly how to do so. Everyone feels love in a unique way, and each of our varied relationships calls us to love differently. Be patient and teach people how to love, since nearly all of us were raised without a full awareness of what love actually is.

Concluding Thoughts

It's extremely important never to expect love from people who are not in alignment. As previously mentioned in *The Vibrational Aura*, alignment means being in harmony with one's mind, body, heart, and spirit. Non-alignment creates a great deal of drama and emotional pain, so individuals temporarily stuck in their funk are unable to be loving towards themselves or anyone else until and unless they pull themselves out of it.

An expectation of receiving unconditional love from people who struggle with self-love and inner peace is irrational. No amount of wishful thinking or falling in love with their potential will ever lead to their ability to give love back. Instead, these unrealistic expectations and wishful thinking often leads to disappointment, frustration, and resentment.

When we accept people fully as they are right now, we become more effective at communicating and setting healthy boundaries. Rather than expecting love and becoming frustrated at its lack of return, we choose to just give love by putting The Love Question into practice. By remaining in our peace and providing peace to others, we naturally help those around us learn how to give and receive love unconditionally, no strings attached.

Tenet Five:
Chaos is an Illusion;
We Seek Harmony

Flashback:

One late night, during the years I operated Earth Spirit Center, I received an email from a man in extreme turmoil. Though the center was closed, I felt guided to make an exception and set an appointment the following day. I had no idea what I was in for. Was it safe? Maybe not, since this man showed signs of a scattered mind filled with hate, prone to harming himself and others. Nonetheless, I knew I had to meet him, and I trusted my gut.

I was alone at the center when he rode in on his motorcycle. When I greeted him, the first thing I noticed were his darting eyes. I also saw that he was carrying a weapon. He said I was his last resort. He was attempting to come off narcotics and was overcome by extreme rage, paranoia, and despair. His path was one of chaotic self-destruction, and his wife and daughter were traumatized by it.

We went into my office and sat on the floor to "ground" ourselves. Every part of his body twitched, and I could tell he was sizing me up. I knew if I judged him in any way, he could easily project all that rage and hatred onto me. Many might say I was wise to be on the defensive with this unstable man, yet all I felt was powerful, overflowing love, peace, and acceptance. I felt safe, a hundred percent secure, and I had only just met him.

We were together for three hours, the first two of which he spent "letting it all out" in a safe space. For the last hour, I asked him to lie down on a reiki table. Then I tuned in with his vibrational aura and offered some energy healing.

We tapped into his heart and found much forgiveness (acceptance) work to be done. I asked him if he could say aloud, "I forgive myself." After about ten minutes he was finally able to do so, and he broke down into tears. His whole demeanor softened as if the tears had washed away all the anger and tension he'd been experiencing. It was a life-transforming moment for him, and for me. It showed me what the power of unconditional acceptance, patience, and kindness can do for someone.

Six months after the session, I received a note from his wife thanking me, expressing that he had been sober for the entire time since his meeting with me. She said his anger issues and general outlook on life had completely changed.

I was filled with happiness upon hearing this news because he wanted to change, and he did. To this day, he says I saved his life. I say he saved his own life since he did the work. I simply provided the safe space for him to do so.

Traditionally, chaos is defined as disorder (physical) and confusion (mental), however, in *Living Peace* we add that chaos is also energetic — our vibrational aura is in turmoil due to the disharmony among our minds, bodies, and hearts. The reason we state "chaos is an illusion" is because it is a pure mental and emotional state (that influences our physical), so we can quickly pierce its delusion and return to peace at any time. The external "chaos" we see out in the world, in individuals or groups, is simply the byproduct of their inner turbulence spilling over, while the perceived "chaos" we see in nature is actually not chaos at all but life's natural balance and flow.

One of the major causes of the perpetuation of chaos is the idea of "chaos" itself. We attach ourselves to the judgments we make in the chaotic present moment, forgetting that life is ever in motion, and that the darkness tonight will be met with the light of the dawn. Every hurricane eventually comes to a standstill, every volcano subsides, and every raging forest fire burns out to give way to new life. The true reality is that balance is always present. It can be found in life if we seek it. It is our job as the living embodiment of peace is to always look beyond the surface level of chaos to find the harmony within.

We can do so through understanding the flow of life. We can choose not to attach ourselves to the mundane or make rash decisions based on temporary emotions or situations. Just like a river, we can go with the flow. Sometimes the current will be smooth, other times it may be rough, but as long as we don't become stagnant, we continue to flow towards greater understanding, and the illusion of chaos doesn't dam the waters of our lives.

Some people find peace in nature, while others find nature to be a harsh world in which there is constant strife and a continual fight for survival. However, nature is a perfect example of balance and harmony. There is no resistance in nature because the plant, animal, and mineral kingdoms have no ego — there is only flow and acceptance of each necessary adaptation. In nature, the essence of harmony is a thriving cooperation among all living things; life and death are just part of the cycle, neither good nor bad. In actuality, we humans are still very much a part of nature. The majority of us may not live in jungles anymore, but we've replaced them with concrete jungles. Even so, the principle of cooperation that brings harmony still holds true, and the principle of releasing resistance also continues to be true. It is when we forget this wisdom that we create suffering for ourselves and others.

We continue our journey toward releasing judgment and resistance by furthering our knowledge and understanding of the world as we peer into chaos. Objectivity is a necessity as we explore this realm of thought; otherwise, we ourselves may become part of the maelstrom. In truth, our minds are the source of most of the chaos we experience in our lives. The stress or drama we feel on a daily basis exists only because of our skewed perceptions of the world which creates our experiences in it. Chaos, like stress, cannot exist unless our thoughts are in agreement with it, or our words and actions are feeding it. When things seem chaotic and groundless, we grab at anything for support and cling tight, which often makes things much worse. It's the primal "flight or fight" reactive behavior that we can learn to intentionally override in our minds and instead choose a course of rational thought and peace.

Chaos is an illusion, we seek harmony — or rather, we cultivate the ability to SEE harmony where the common eye cannot. As discussed earlier in this book, our egoic mind has a tendency to make sense of the world by compartmentalizing things as "good" and "bad", "right" and "wrong". Often, this dualism is what creates or magnifies inner and outer chaos. For example, when our flight or fight mode is activated due to fear, it becomes far too easy to react in blind haste rather than respond with mindful grace. Whenever we are not self-contained and self-composed, we ultimately add further pain to the world by throwing our words around, spilling our fear, anger, or any number of separating vibrations onto all that is around us.

The Spilling Effect:

What happens when you bleed and don't attend to your wound? You spill blood onto anything you touch. The same applies to our personal energy, vibration, and degree of consciousness. If we are in fear, we spill fear. If we are in anger or grief, we spill anger or grief. Whatever mental or emotional pain we are experiencing, we spill that pain onto the people and into the environment in which we currently abide. We're like individual micro suns in our personal galaxy of life — we may shed ample light, withhold it, or possibly produce so much intensity that we incinerate everything around us. So, what does all this have to do with chaos? Chaos is the byproduct of our human egos — the part of ourselves that's unable to allow life to flow its natural course.

Instead, our egos make us feel we must control our world (and those in it), and that's when chaos is created.

The greatest irony is that we as humans don't need to fight each other — we choose to. Due to our egoic nature, we constantly find new ways to go to W.A.R. (We Are Right!) even in times of peace. In our biased perceptions we knowingly or unknowingly support war-mongering leaders who get our adrenaline pumping while validating our fears and prejudices. We must always remember that peace cannot arise from war. Killing or fighting and harmony or happiness aren't matching vibrations. However, the silver lining in times of conflict, whether personal or global, is that they highlight our chaotic tendencies more than ever, especially in the parts of ourselves we hide because we deem them ugly: prejudice, racism, or blind hatred. If our choices lead to harm, whether emotional or physical in our homes, or through the institutions and leaders we support, we then know very clearly that we support suffering. However, if our choices build bridges of compassion and understanding, we can rest in the knowledge that karmic patterns are being healed even if the results aren't seen immediately.

There is much more power in peace, acceptance, and allowing than there is in resistance. Many people applaud and see resistance as strength, when it's actually stagnation that causes Dis-Ease of mind, body, and spirit. A resistant mind is a closed mind; a resistant body is a sick body; and a resistant spirit is a dim spirit. When the mind holds onto Dis-Ease and resists change, its thoughts create suffering. The body has natural ways of self-cleansing, all of which allow Dis-Ease to flow out of the body. When our bodies become stagnant and the flow is blocked, sickness manifests. When we resist the natural call of our human connection with harmony and kindness, it can result in rage, depression, and even suicide. Everything that brings us wellbeing is achieved by allowing ourselves to flow with and be in harmony with life. So why do we so strongly feel we must control everyone and everything? Why does everyone have to believe and behave the same as we do before we feel safe and secure? The answers to all these questions are: Because of its delusions, our egos need to push, pull, or hold tight.

It is of vital importance we learn the art of allowing all life, including other people, to "just be". Throughout history, tampering with cultures and ecosystems has caused much harm. In the microcosm, we can see how tampering with the lives of our loved ones can actually push them further into pain, addiction, and feelings of separation. In fact, "tampering" might be seen as another word for "judgment". We feel we are right and "justified" in meddling, forgetting it's only ever our job to listen, understand, and hold space for them — not be their savior. In other words, we must learn to allow all things to grow in their own time. Tender care without judgment and tampering IS possible, and when we care for ourselves and others with patience and mindfulness, harmony much like that which exists in nature can be found. People are not weeds to be pulled, nor are their unsightly qualities meant to be ripped out. Trying to force change only leads to further chaos. Instead, we allow, we watch, and we offer support — and with this peaceful approach, we begin to notice that each person bears a unique and beautiful blossom of their own. We also understand that not everyone will be nourished the same in the same soil.

Let's ask ourselves: Have we built the foundation of our lives on the shifting sands of a beach? Each night the tide comes in, pushing sand away from our foundation. Each morning when the tide rolls back out, we rebuild, using more sand to provide a buffer for the coming tides. This is the story of our lives — the tide rolls in at night to wash away our foundation, and each morning we exert more energy to rebuild it. Our lives become all about maintaining what we've built, and there's no energy left with which to expand and build something more. When all the while, we could have simply chosen to accept reality and let the ocean reclaim the sand that always belonged to it. We chose to build upon the ocean's territory, resisting the reality that sand at the shore of the ocean is not a stable foundation upon which to build. A beach is beautiful, yes, but it's instability isn't suitable for building a solid foundation.

Do we accept reality and act accordingly? Or do we resist or deny it, trying to fight impermanence by pretending that change isn't occurring? In nature, the species that is most capable of adapting thrives. Pain will happen in life, yet it is our attachment to the pain and our resistance to change that causes suffering.

What is realized in this mastery is that the violent lightning storms of our lives are all created from our own "negative" (separating, disharmonious) energy.

The visual is running around trying to extinguish the little fires that keep spreading after the lightning strikes. When we extinguish one, another instantly springs up, so we are never able put them all out. This is because the friction of our rash movements creates more fires. If we simply slowed down and responded from a place of calm deliberation, we could douse all the fires without creating more.

When we're aware and in control of our energy, and we embody peace, the storm subsides. Instead, most people fear the lightning, as if it's something outside themselves. They don't realize that what they run from is within them, so wherever they go the storm will follow. The more fearful, angry, stressed, or depressed the person becomes, the more powerful the storm grows. Hating the storm or judging the storm doesn't help. Only peace will calm it, and that peace must come from within.

Our experienced reality is often a mirror, reflecting back to us the optimism, neutrality, or pessimism that dwells in our subconscious minds. It's important to remember that perception alters reality, as we covered in *Mastery if Thought*. Perception forms a Mental Overlay over the physical landscape of our experiences. Everything in life is neutral, yet it is our mind, or rather our egos, that project the Mental Overlay that colors everything with duality, creating conflict and chaos between our hearts and minds.

If the above teaching is still difficult to absorb, look no further than three siblings, similar in age, all growing up in the same dysfunctional family. Although there are some similarities among them, what's fascinating to observe is the difference of outcome in their lives. One sibling may rise out of the dysfunction while the other two remain caught up in it. Looking closer, we see that each child's perception of life plays a vital role in their personal outcome. Perception can be influenced but not forced, it is first inherent then self-created as we mature. This is why kids from abusive families can still turn out to be very happy and successful, and why kids coming from happy, supportive families end up with depression and suicidal tendencies. Environment has a major influence, yes; yet it ultimately comes down to what's happening in each child's mind, how they perceive, absorb and then project their reality. The beauty in this is that we eventually learn to create and alter our mental landscape ourselves as adults — transforming any past pain into lives of happiness and peace.

≫ ≫ ≫ ≪ ≪ ≪

Our call to action is to be in the flow of life, accepting

reality as it is, and as it comes. We must allow life to "be" in all its impermanent grandeur. Nothing remains the same, and those who fight change, or are in denial of it, create chaos in their own lives and the lives of those they have influence over.

When there is excessive fire, we must be water, to soothe. When there is excess water, we must be earth, to absorb and nourish. When there is excess earth (or overabundant weeds), we must be fire to purge, motivate and promote change. Chaos is illusion, since it is only a reality we create when we fight against the flow of life. Harmony can be found and nurtured in any situation — and it's our choice where we place our focus each day.

A monk was sitting by a river, enjoying its natural beauty and serenity. Two men on the nearby road could be heard arguing over the existence of God. The monk, unconcerned with the argument, continued to enjoy the world's natural splendor around him, while the two men were completely oblivious to Life passing them by as they argued. Blinded by their need to be heard and to be right, they couldn't see or feel the peace available to them at that moment, in every moment.

Practice 5
The River
(Chaos is an Illusion;
We Seek Harmony)

The River is all about honoring both the rapids and the calm flow of life. One minute, we might be drifting down the lazy river, and the next, we might be met with raging waters. The goal is to not lose our peace and balance, which upsets our boat. The worst thing we can do is panic and grab for a nearby rock or log out of fear of going any further. If we allow ourselves to stagnate in reaction to the chaos of our lives, minor pain turns into its lingering form—chronic suffering. If we allow ourselves to flow through the rapids, we might still experience pain, but its discomfort will be brief, as we navigate through it, often to find ourselves right back in the river's lazy flow. It's our choice to cling and keep ourselves imperiled in the rapids or dare to let go, go with the flow, and see what's around the next bend in the river.

A great analogy to use here: actual river rafting instructions—If you fall into the rapids, immediately turn and float on your back with your feet pointing downstream. Don't attempt to stand up, even in shallow rapids, or your feet or legs may get stuck or beaten up by rocks. Floating on your back with your feet guiding you allows you to flow over and around the large rocks, and you can use your feet to push yourself off any obstacles you might otherwise bump into. Within moments, the other rafters will pull you aboard. Note: This did happen to one of my fellow rafters when I went on a rapids rafting trip years ago!

The Practice

When you experience disarray or discomfort, remind

yourself that chaos is simply a perspective, an illusion, and peace can be arrived at from within at any time. Envision yourself in the river and decide whether you are clinging or flowing. Another visual is to see yourself in the eye of the storm, watching the chaos whirling all around you, yet not touching you. It is your choice to enter into the storm, or remain the calm in its center until it passes. Often, people try to fight against the contrast of their lives, and it's always as futile as yelling at a hurricane to stop blowing. Storms need to run their course, and the same applies to the metaphoric storms of our lives that are fueled by stress, frustration, grief, and anger. When we embody the peace and allow the storms of our lives to bypass us, they need not affect us in a "negative way". Pain happens, but suffering is optional. Chaos is an illusion, and we can master it by being the harmonizing force within the storm.

What to do:

Whenever there is contrast in your life; let it go. Flow with the river rather than against it. Cool the volcano. Sit in the eye of the tornado. Leave town during a hurricane. Do not resist or fight against the storms of your life, just allow them to pass on by. Be the harmony, and you'll see amazing results, results that include having more energy left over. With this energy, you can pick up any pieces that fell out of place, or, it may be that you have fewer pieces to pick up because you didn't participate in the chaos!

Sometimes the storm may strike directly at you, but if so, you must remain calm. Remember, your emotional state of being fuels the storm. When another person is throwing metaphoric "hot coals" at you, allow them to bounce off you. Never grab the coal and throw it back, or you, too, get burned. If you continue moving forward, you'll soon be beyond the reach of the person throwing coals.

Accessing Your River's Flow

Each day, preferably in the morning, when you take time out for meditation and contemplation — reflect on the direction of your internal river. Is it in harmony, flowing smooth and steady? Or is there turbulence, splashing its waters in every direction? Or is it stagnant, with little to no movement — simply pooling and then evaporating with nowhere to go? Meditate on and contemplate your river — practicing this visualization and the energetic feeling of it. This river is vibrational in essence, much like your vibrational aura, since it is the accumulation of your thoughts, emotions, and choices.

If you are calm, chances are the river flows smooth. If you are worked up or distracted, it is likely tossing lots of water on its banks. If you are feeling numb or depressed, your river will likely be unmoving, and Dis-Ease is festering beneath the surface.

A River of Thoughts

It's important knowing exactly where your energy flows each day. Keeping a daily journal of your thoughts and emotions will help you determine what's predominantly on your mind. It will also allow you to reflect on the week and month. You'll soon recognize a pattern when you keep it consistently. This pattern is more easily recognized when you write, instead of just mentally contemplating your thoughts and actions. Writing makes your pattern concrete, so you are less likely to ignore it.

By diligently applying the previous four tenet practices to your life, you'll gain the ability to direct your vibrational river's flow, rather than allowing it to stagnate, spill over onto others, or scatter in all directions — depleting your own vitality (your chi or Ki life force, as some call it).

Recognize the flow then direct the flow. It doesn't matter what's happening in your outer world; this is a purely internal practice of observation and cultivated self-discipline.

While it's true that your river is the outward flow of energy you direct into the world, it also flows within you and affects you just as much as it does others. Like it or not, our energy always influences both ourselves and others, which is why this practice of greater mindfulness and self-direction is so crucial.

Tenet Six:
Duality is an Illusion;
We Seek Transcendence

Flashback:

I really enjoy working with teenagers who are eager to learn, and most of them are incredible knowledge sponges when given the opportunity to soak up new ideas. One such experience I had was with a very special, intelligent girl who was fourteen years old when we first met.

A colleague of mine recommended me as a teen coach for this girl. Her mother had tried everything she knew to do with no results, and, like the man from the previous chapter, I was her last resort before she planned to admit her daughter to a mental hospital.

Four months prior to our meeting, this young lady began burning her body using ice and salt. She didn't know why she inflicted these wounds on herself; her parents certainly had no clue, and all the therapists they took her to weren't finding any answers. Three months of therapy had resolved nothing. Meanwhile, the girl continued to sink deeper into depression, feeling more and more isolated and judged, which perpetuated her self-mutilation.

When she arrived and sat down in my office for the first time, all I saw was beauty. I shared my approach to healing with her and her mother, and they both felt comfortable and at ease with my philosophy. Then I sent Mom on her merry way, so her daughter and I could get down to business.

*Not once did I tell the girl she needed to stop burning herself, nor did I say it was "bad". I really **didn't** think it was "bad" — that was the key. I didn't express judgments, nor did I even have them in my thoughts. Again, all I saw was beauty. I realized she just wasn't satisfied or happy, so we focused all our attention on bringing greater satisfaction and happiness into her daily life. Each time we met, she revealed more layers of her misery to me, and each time I sent her home with more FEEL-GOOD homework to do. There were a few relapses that she filled me in on, but after only two months she went from a 0-1 happiness rating (her words) to an 8-9. Her urge to* *burn herself was gone. By teaching her how to use the tools we're covering in this book, she turned her life around in a short period of time.*

Students and clients alike repeatedly tell me that they believe what makes the *Living Peace* teachings so distinct is the emphasis on non-duality. Although non-dualistic wisdom is subtly alluded to in our modern era — and has been taught for centuries in esoteric formats — it's rare to find anyone who teaches nonduality in a simple, clear and concise manner. That said, dear reader, this tenet is of vital importance to understand. Unless we transcend (rise above) duality, inner peace can never be attained.

What is duality? "Duality" means that everything is dual and has a polar opposite. This encompasses light to dark, masculine to feminine, love to hate, hot to cold, East to West, Yin to Yang, and so on, *ad infinitum*. Ancient mystical teachings from all over the world allow us to understand that these supposedly "polar opposites" are just varying degrees of the same thing, on the same continuum. In reality, there is no point where cold ends and hot begins; they are both just degrees of temperature. Our perceptions define the duality involved. For the purpose of this book, we'll only look at the aspects of duality that deal with "negative" judgment, such as what is "bad", "evil", "dark", "wrong", etc.

Understanding Duality & Polarity

I've come to teach a distinction between polarity and duality. Polarity is the inherent dichotomy found throughout the Universe. It exists in all things, down to our very atoms with their positive and negative particles. This polarity exists naturally in our world as daytime and nighttime, hot and cold, and even birth and death. Anytime two seemingly opposing forces are found, there's likely a polarity involved in which one cannot exist without the other. This creates a healthy balance so Life may flourish. Taoists may recognize this beautiful harmonizing dance via the Yin and Yang symbol, in which each contrast organically flows into the other, forever waxing and waning.

In natural polarity there is no judgment involved. Nothing is bad or wrong, it just exists. The moment we begin to add judgment, opinion, and morality to Life (such as viewing the darkness of nighttime as "scary", or death as something "terrible") we humans create duality. In order to make sense of the world, we develop opinions about what is good, what is bad, what is right, and what is wrong. We may even develop our own opposing concepts such as what is holy or sinful, or the dualism of heaven and hell. Because these opinions are all based on human perception and assumptions—this human-made duality causes our planet more harm than benefit.

An important reminder: As long as there is a group of people who believe that they are right, and all others are wrong, humans will continue to inflict pain and separation upon each other and on the Earth.

Duality & Manipulation

Traditionally, duality means something that is two-sided. However, in the *Living Peace* teachings, I find it optimal to provide a meaning that better helps us distinguish duality from polarity. As stated above, polarity is the inherent polarizing aspects of nature, while duality is our human ego adding amoral and moral, likes and dislikes, etc. etc. to our human existence. It even separates the Mundane from the spiritual in life.

Duality, at its core, is a form of manipulation and an ego reinforcer. Because we see the world through a dualistic lens of good and bad, right and wrong, we harshly judge ourselves and others. Many unknowingly becoming emotional and spiritual abusers because they feel led by divine justice to do so.

When we live with a perspective that sees only black and white with no gray areas permitted, we become lazy in our thinking and just reiterate what we think is right, instead of taking the time to fully understand every situation as unique and deserving of deeper discernment. Even parenting may become lazy. For instance, instead of fully explaining why an activity is harmful, we may tell our child that it's "bad" or "wrong" to do. Smoking isn't "bad" or "wrong", but it does have a lot of health risks associated with it. However, say a teen does begin to smoke—subconsciously they may feel immense guilt and shame, believing that smoking is "bad"; therefore, they must be "bad" since ego tends to make these kinds of assumptions. Furthermore, a parent lacking control over their impulses and emotions may find out their teen is smoking and call him or her a "bad kid" in their anger, which adds to the negative narrative being developed in their child's subconscious mind. This causes the teen to have feelings of immense separation.

People who've been told they are "bad" or "sinful", and can't do anything "right", develop powerful beliefs in their subconscious minds that keep them trapped in toxic behavior and relationships. Addiction, for example, carries with it immense guilt. Those who are addicted are often aware of its negative impact on themselves and others, yet their low self-worth keeps them "using". Drugs or other substances have become the coping mechanism that "enables" them to handle the heavy weight of guilt, shame, and pain that they carry. Society screaming that it's "bad and wrong" to do what they're doing—or worse, yelling that they're "a disappointment" and "bad and wrong" for being addicts is of zero percent help and actually has the reverse effect of furthering their dualistic feelings of separation.

Disclaimer: *In the upcoming section, when I use LOVE, it's a simple, catch-all word for being in alignment with peace, choosing compassion, harmony, and understanding over dualistic mindsets that propagate further separation and all the "negative" emotions that come with it.*

≫ ≫ ≫ ≪ ≪ ≪

Positive energy is unifying energy, while negative energy is separating energy — and an easy analogy (from *Mastery of Thought*) is to imagine our hearts drifting closer or further away from one another depending on our thoughts, beliefs, and the words and actions we undertake on a regular basis.

Picture every person you deem "bad" then apply to each the belief that they've created a reality in which they are separate from LOVE and the hearts of others. This separation may be an illusion, yet to them it is reality, and it causes them deep suffering which manifests itself in projecting their pain onto those around them. As a reminder, **people who suffer the most often inflict the most pain onto others.** We can certainly find compassion for these individuals as well as understanding for ourselves when, we too, fall into the role of "abuser" due to our suffering. Healing occurs when we remove the judgment involved and begin considering the solution rather than the problem. We acknowledge the feelings of separation and embrace the wisdom that only LOVE can bring anyone back into alignment. And unconditional LOVE can only exist when we embody peace.

This is where many in the world miss the mark. Instead of using LOVE to assist in bringing people back into alignment, we punish "bad" people and lock them away, creating further separation and further reinforcement of the reality that they actually are "bad." There is no such thing as a "bad" person; we are all here to learn and grow. What does exist are people who feel so far removed from the heart that, to them, love doesn't even exist—many of them having been raised in and surrounded by **conditional** love, if any love at all. This causes deep-seated illusions of separation. Peace starts within the home as the foundation that LOVE thrives upon. Unconditional LOVE is the outward expression of inner peace. Let me repeat that: **Unconditional LOVE is the outward expression of inner peace.** Read it again please: **Unconditional love is the outward expression of inner peace.** This is crucial to understand!

Let's take a moment to review loving actions as we previously explored in *Practice: The Love Question*. **Love is:** kindness, respect, appreciation, honesty, compassion, listening, understanding, and acceptance. **Love exists in:** joyful and peaceful being, laughter, dignity, grace, sharing happiness, and unattachment (freedom). Please always remember that, energetically, judgment and love cannot exist in the same place at the same time. We are invited to forever hone our awareness to ensure that the LOVE we are providing is a love that encourages each individual to feel free, supported, heard, and appreciated. In other words, it's important to leave our own attachments, biases, and personal agendas behind.

Note: A common question I receive from new students is, "What about people who commit atrocious crimes, such as taking another person's life? How do you not view them as bad!?"

My response, "Their actions were of extreme violence and created suffering in the world. I don't need to label them dualistically to speak of the facts involved. For me to view them as "bad" or "evil" would only cultivate further separation in the world, including within my heart. Instead, I view their actions factually — free from opinion — so that I may foster a heart of compassion for every person impacted by their violent choices, including the perpetrator."

If we take a close look into the heart of any person who commits violent crimes against humanity and our planet, we will find a disconnect from reality (delusion), a separation from love, a heart filled with pain or even completely numb of all feeling. Our history books aren't filled with people who believe themselves to be "bad" or "evil"; instead, every person who's hurt others has had a motive or reason that they believed was "justified". The motives someone has stem from "negative" emotion and a mind filled with separation. Therefore, concerning ourselves with whether people are "good" or "bad" is a fruitless endeavor. Instead, we can choose to focus our energy on mending the hearts and minds of humanity so these atrocities cease to occur. How do we achieve this goal? By seeing beyond ignorance, chaos, and duality in order that we may embody peace and then teach peace to our children. Together, we can create a reality in which no child ever grows into an adult without a heart that knows love and a mind that knows peace.

Practice 6
The Eraser
(Duality is an Illusion;
We Seek Transcendence)

This is an excellent practice to cultivate for the rest of your life. It erases dualistic vocabulary from our minds, especially the "negative." The first step is to stop saying specific words, and the second step is to stop thinking these words.

I can always tell when a student or client is in duality based on the words they use. When my students reach a certain stage in their growth and practice, I invite them to cease using dualistic words to describe people, situations, and energy.

This practice was illustrated brilliantly for me when a longtime student of mine found herself not feeling well and began noticing her increased frustration with people. She wanted to love them and be a vessel for healing, yet people as a whole irritated her. As we talked, I noticed she continuously used the words "light" and "dark". I invited her to change her vocabulary and remember that the very essence of the Universe is Love, that everything IS of the "light" and there is no separation between what is "light" and what is "dark"; it's simply the value our egos place on it. She readily accepted this practice. The next day she was back in alignment and feeling great. The reason she felt unwell was because her ego continued to separate her from others via her thoughts of duality over who was of the light and who was of the dark. The moment she released the judgments she realigned with peace and unity. It's excellent to remember that the duality and separation we judge in the world is ultimately mirrored as separation in ourselves.

The Practice

Here are some words — used in a "negative" way — to

begin erasing from your vocabulary: "dark," "bad," "sin," "evil," "shadow," "ego," "low vibration," "I hate," "I don't like," "poor," "negative," "hard," "can't," etc. This list is by no means complete, feel free to add others as they occur to you, and strive to limit their use until full cessation occurs.

This is a great practice because it forces us to more often use neutral or positive words to describe things in our life. We don't realize how judgmental and separating we are most of the time. When we intentionally change our vocabularies, it shows us just how often we use dualistic words in a negative context. And even when we may not be using or intending them in a "negative" context, they still hold power and vibration, thus they influence our lives.

As you journey through this practice, continue to erase any other adjectives that you use to describe things you're in resistance to. When you cease to talk or think about things "negatively," you cease to emit separating energy. Please note that this is **not** denying the truth of reality at all — in actuality, speaking more neutrally and factually embraces the truer reality since we're eliminating the dualistic opinions about our life situations.

Removing "I don't like" and "I hate"

It's very helpful to remove *"I don't like"* and *"I hate"* from your vocabulary, whether spoken or thought. Find new ways to express your preferences. Instead, practice saying, "That's not my highest preference" or "Thank you, but I prefer _____." Key word here is preference. We don't need hard likes and dislikes to exist and have our own personalities; we are quite capable of soft preferences that are inspiration-based rather than judgment-based.

Please note: There are people who very much like the

things we don't like since the world is such a diverse place. Sometimes, when we speak of hating or disliking something, we're talking in front of someone who may find joy and benefit in that very thing! When we judge the things we don't prefer, it can come across as rude or even belittling. However, when it comes to things that are harmful to yourself and others, the way to bring people back to peace isn't by judging their behavior, it's by asking questions and fostering understanding. "I hate that you did that!" is unhelpful, whereas "Can you please explain what led you to do that?" brings understanding, connection, and healing.

Removing "need" and "should"

It's also extremely helpful to erase "need" and "should" from your vocabulary when talking to other people and telling them they "need" to do or "should "do something. No one ever "needs" to do anything you say, and "should-ing" on people is just another form of judgment. These two words create separation since they project biased expectations and eventual disappointments within yourself and others.

Please be sure to also cease "should-ing" on yourself! Instead of saying "I need to do this" or "I should do that" change your vocabulary to fact-based sentences instead of judgment-based sentences. Examples: "It would be healthy for me to do this" or "It would help me achieve my goals quicker if I did that".

Rather than telling people what they "need" to do, offer invitations. "I invite you to _____" is a wonderful way to share helpful perspectives and suggestions, giving the other person the freedom of choice instead of your expectations. "I invite myself to" works in the same fashion. This helps remove personal guilt if you set a plan and didn't follow through. Guilt is not a helpful motivator! That's why you feel "bad" when you don't do as you "should". "Should-ing" and the guilt it creates depletes energy.

A final thought:

What about the "positives" of duality, such as light and goodness, etc.?

Those words are fine when we use them in an uplifting way, not comparing in a way that separates. For example, "I am the light in the darkness" still alludes to duality, while "Everything is of the light and our goal is to shine uniquely, each in our own beautiful way" helps transcend duality. I, personally, do not use words such as light or dark, instead choosing to speak more literally. My alterative to: "I am here to heal others and be a bright light in the world" is "Each day, I choose to respond from a place of peace and practice compassion for all." This still achieves the goal of the first sentence, is less ego-assertive, and instead comes from a place of non-duality. However, I do meet students and clients where they are at in their layer of consciousness by using words that are relevant for them, as in the case of my student struggling with judgments of who was "light" and who was "dark".

Part Three:

The Three Attachments

The Power of Meditation

As we ready ourselves to release the Three Attachments, it's important to take this pause and discuss meditation. So far, much of what's been learned has been a form of active mindfulness. Now that you have the initial six teachings under your belt, it's time to strengthen your peace practice by transforming your active mindfulness into daily meditation practice. Without consistent meditation, the Three Attachments will be increasingly difficult to fully release.

Many people go into meditation with the idea that they must have a quiet mind. This is not "true". A tranquil mind may eventually occur as a by-product of consistent meditation over time, yet the main goal of meditation is to first learn self-discipline of the body by sitting still each day. If you go into meditation practice expecting an instantly quiet mind, it's easy to get frustrated and give up. However, if you go into meditation accepting the busy mind for what it is, and just practice sitting still—this is much more doable. Additionally, the practice of intentional daily "sitting" helps us develop greater consistency, structure, and self-discipline—which, in turn, further encourages our understanding and application of each tenet.

Although there are many forms of meditation, each style usually falls into one of two categories—concentration and contemplation, or as I like to call them, Still Mind and Observant Mind. In **Still Mind** we literally take a pause, ceasing any analysis or absorption of information or energy. To achieve this, we may anchor our focus by using an image, a mantra, or simply concentrating on our breath. In **Observant Mind** meditation, we actively come into the presence of our aliveness—using this time to notice all things that rise up and eventually recede within us. We embrace and accept every thought, feeling and emotion that may arise while still practicing unattachment. The goal of **Observant Mind** is to fully take on the role of the neutral observer behind our mind, ego, personality, and Self.

Still Mind allows us to strengthen our self-discipline, willpower and resolve, while **Observant Mind** grants us priceless insights into the inner workings of our subconscious. Together, both meditation styles help us become more attuned to life by developing a strong foundation of mindfulness and undivided presence. **Self-discipline is mindfulness in action.**

A helpful mantra to use before or during meditation is:

> *Beyond thought: I am not my thoughts*
> *Beyond feeling: I am not my feelings*
> *Beyond emotion: I am not my emotions*
>   *I am the awareness behind my mind*
>   *I am the awareness behind my body*
>   *I am the awareness behind my heart*
> *I am the eternal observer*
> *And breath is my anchor*

Originally, in Hinduism and Buddhism, mantras were used as a word or sound repeatedly spoken to assist concentration in meditation. Today, mantras may also be repeated slogans or positive affirmations that act as useful reminders to invoke beneficial change.

As you begin meditation, it's best to be seated on the floor, so you are "grounded", with the best posture you can achieve. However, the primary goal is not perfection, merely to practice and follow through. If you need to be in a chair or have oodles of cushions for support, by all means do what's most comfortable and will allow meditation to occur. For those who choose to push themselves into more traditional postures of meditation, it is helpful to note that slight discomfort is normal. As the days continue, your body will grow accustomed to the posture, and the discomfort will lessen. Set a timer for five minutes and increase by a minute each day (or every couple of days) until you reach twenty minutes per day. When the timer goes off during each meditation session, you're welcome to continue meditating, but do not arise before the timer rings. This will help you develop self-discipline and stick-with-it-ness!

I recommend starting off with at least five minutes of **Still Mind** meditation, followed by five minutes of **Observant Mind** meditation. Have a pen and journal nearby to jot down afterward any awarenesses that may manifest during each sitting.

By consciously slowing down, we strengthen our resolve, and by activating our resolve we pierce the veil of our delusions.

Here are some additional **Still Mind** and **Observant Mind** ways to invoke meditation daily:

> It is sunrise — I take a moment of appreciation
> It is midday — I take a moment of pause
> It is dusk — I take a moment of appreciation
> It is night — I take a moment of pause

Morning Appreciation:

Reflect on the beauty of being alive — having 24 brand new hours to participate in. Rather than feeling the weight of any upcoming responsibilities you may have during the day ahead, replace the begrudging "I have to" with "I get to". The statement "I get to" releases resistance and activates the ultimate truth: Being alive is miraculous. So, no matter what you do, or accomplish, you are enough because *being alive is enough.* Free from resistance, you begin to walk with lighter steps and feel a growing peace.

*Note: Morning appreciation is also a wonderful time to express morning gratitudes. Be sure to activate your appreciation for life and your aliveness. Remember that you are **alive**, and this blessing is the greatest of all. Twenty-four brand new hours to enjoy and share your life with others! How will you use them?*

Midday Pause:

Around noon, or during your lunch break, take three to five minutes to literally "take a break". We hear the phrase *"lunch break"* yet how many of us actually use that time to momentarily pause and slow down our minds, allowing them to rest and recharge? Rather than immediately checking your phone, social media, picking up a fun novel, squeezing in additional planning for the day, or enjoying lunch with colleagues or friends—allow your mind silence. Ideally, find someplace quiet where you can close your eyes and sit for a few minutes without any other agenda on your mind. If you're unable to "get away" during this time, simply let the people around you know that you will be taking a few minutes of silence. After awhile, it will become second nature for others to respect your space.

Please remember that even doing something you enjoy still takes energy, so providing your mind and body a time of non-action and non-stimulation each day is especially rejuvenating.

Note: if meditation happens naturally – great! However, do not force it during these times of pause. Sometimes, the mind grasps at what it thinks meditation "should" look or feel like and self-criticizes. Just sit and be with your Self – no extra sounds, no music, no guided meditation, just the sounds of life happening around you – for these few minutes. Also, don't be offended or bothered by the sounds of life, accept them. Just breathe, allowing all things to simply be without adding opinion one way or another.

Twilight Appreciation:

Reflect on the impermanence of being alive, realizing everything is temporary, brief and beautiful--like a flower. Notice how quickly the day went by, how quickly all days go by. Are you fully aware of how much life passes you by each week, each month, each year? Take every day's twilight time to remember and appreciate the miracle of aliveness. If you can be outside during this time to watch the sun set, please do so. Watch the final day's rays of light fall upon the earth. Observe the birds winging their way home for the night and other critters awakening to forage. Listen to the sound of insects beginning to stir with the cooling temperatures, or, in winter, listen to the brisk silence.

Note: Perhaps you're driving home in rush hour traffic. Turn the radio off for a few minutes and allow yourself to accept the backup of traffic. Look beyond the vehicles to see the many lives each car represents. So many people, yet such harmony as everyone works together in a structured fashion to make their way home. If there's an accident and traffic slows even more, send compassion not frustration. Release your own desire to be home sooner and accept the current reality of where you are – making it a time of present reflection and grace. Become alive to the life around you – seeing it fully through unbiased eyes, without adding stories or opinions. Simply observe, and appreciate all life happening around you.

Nightly Pause:

It is time to take your break fully and lay the day you had down. No more mulling over its events or conversations in your mind. Now is the time to let go and sink into a state of rest. Your nightly pause invites intentional stillness and silence. This is a perfect opportunity to meditate, take a bath, sit by candlelight, and you might pray, journal or read spiritual material afterwards for a spell. Nightly Pause is a time to care for your body, let your mind rest, and nourish your soul — not a time to analyze or try to squeeze in any new activities or stimulations.

Concluding Thoughts

It's often the simple daily practices that influence our lives in dramatic ways. Most people would never go a day without brushing their teeth, and we're all aware of the long-term health consequences of not brushing daily. We don't think, "Oh, well, my teeth are great, so I don't need to brush for awhile!" We realize it's the daily brushing that keeps teeth healthy. Likewise, the wise mystics of our time would never go a day without practicing meditation and introspection. To achieve a state of wisdom and peace we must meditate, and to maintain that state, we must meditate some more. Meditation is a form medication.

Brushing for your dental health is like meditating for your mental health.

If we want to see results, we must do the work. This is the single most important awareness that many people toss aside. There's a misconception floating around that, once we get to a certain point in our growth, we don't need to continue to maintain it. However, wise masters know that practice is always necessary because only the present moment contains life, thus what was learned yesterday no longer exists. A little story by way of illustration is this: The student asks the wise yogi how to become more centered in body and mind and the yogi responds, "Practice yoga." Then the student asks how he,

too, can become a yogi one day, and the yogi responds,
"Practice yoga every day for the rest of your life."

Tenet Seven:

Release the Mundane

Flashback:

Disclaimer:
In the following paragraphs a lot of seemingly "negative" things will be listed; however, please observe that I'm just noting them – they are not complaints or gripes, only matter-of-fact events. Later, they are revealed as beautiful experiences that helped me Release the Mundane.

June 1, 2018

My husband, Andrew, and I moved to Bayfield, Colorado to start our conjoined lives and establish our new business, The Zen Cowboy. We bought some land and a commercial building in historic downtown at a great price; however, the remodeling cost to turn it into a commercial residence was three times as much as expected. What we thought would cost 10-15K and take one month to complete, took five months and well over 30K, which ate up all of our savings.

For the three months of remodeling, the building was a total construction zone. I primarily slept on an air mattress in what's now the kitchen near two big holes that had been jack-hammered through the concrete slab to reach the plumbing for a commercial restroom and residential shower. Dust and dirt covered everything. We had no floor except for a small carpet remnant in the little backroom where Andrew slept on two couches pushed together. I went without a shower or bath for just over five weeks, taking what I called "raccoon baths" in the sink of our powder room.

To paint the picture even more vividly, during our first month in Colorado, I experienced severe pain in my throat, had chronic fatigue and I couldn't speak. I'd contracted laryngitis, which lasted nearly four weeks. More personally, I also had burning hemorrhoids that manifested right after our long drive from Arizona. These also persisted the whole month due to my inability to bathe properly. (Epson Salts baths help a lot!)

I remember lying on the makeshift bed of two couches, just starting at a beige wall in physical agony, feeling trapped in our demolished space since we couldn't continue construction for another two months. (We were awaiting proper permits and inspections.) Tears of pain and anger bled from my eyes as I realized I had zero control or power in this situation. Nothing I could do would change any of it — there was no relief from the burning I felt top to bottom (quite literally) and no relief from the uncomfortable disarray of our living space. I felt like jumping off a bridge, or just falling asleep to never wake up again — at least then the constant pain would be gone. Of course, those thoughts didn't last long, but you get the idea!

Despite all our pain, frustration and discomfort, my husband and I never spoke out of alignment towards each other. We were a perfect team of support. Some days, I held the torch of peace; other days, he did, and we maintained our equilibrium when communicating with everyone involved in our project. We did an amazing job of coping. No blame, no shame — although there were fleeting moments of anger or depression (as described above). Mostly, we were in a state of graceful acceptance. After all, both Andrew and I actively practice the Living Peace teachings, so we well understand that wanting reality to be different than what it is (resistance) is a major source of suffering.

The reason I share the above story is that — for my entire life up to this point was filled with creature comforts — a nice bed, warm showers, a floor that wasn't dirt beneath my feet, etc. When all of these were taken away; it forced me into the minimalistic lifestyle of a monastic monk. 95% of my belongings were still in storage. Additionally, I was unable to work and had no choice but to take a sabbatical from my teaching, coaching, and community. So, with everything familiar I knew gone, including the role I'd grown so fond of as teacher, who was I? Ungrounded, without my familiar Self, I let go and found comfort in not knowing, releasing any attachments to the person I had thought myself to be.

Mundane: tangible, material; of this earthly world

When we fully come to the release of our mundane attachments, all of our complaints seem to naturally fade away. This is excellent news because the reason behind the cessation of our grievances is that we have become less bothered by life as a whole.

There is a very old eastern story of a man who tried covering the world with leather so as to not step on any thorns. One day, another man asked him why he didn't just make himself a pair of leather shoes!

When we are attached to the Mundane world, everything is likely to trouble us, and we may even fear the thorns that are inevitable in life. As mentioned in the 5 Layers of Consciousness, those in the Mundane and Collective see the world through the dualistic lenses of "good" and "bad" and "right" and "wrong". Someone attached to the Mundane will likely try to change it (cover the world with leather) in order to be comfortable, rather than realizing (as in the Transcendent and Galactic) that all exterior comfort is fleeting while lasting inner comfort (peace) can only be found within.

As we've been learning throughout this book (and noted in the Living Peace Code), "Everything is impermanent; change is the only constant." Releasing the Mundane honors the truth of impermanence. How can we ever be fully attached to anyone or anything? Becoming so is impossible, really, because nothing stays the same forever. Nonetheless, we do become attached, and we do feel the pain of loss because of this futile attachment. This wisdom is a tough pill to swallow because it means all our mental and emotional pain is self-inflicted — often our physical pain, too, since our mind has such a strong influence on our body!

The pain we feel in life often leads to one of three outcomes, or a combination of the three. First, we push down our emotions and become so hardened by the world that we act hard towards the world in return. The second outcome is that we become an emotional puddle melting under the pain of life into tears and sorrow, often withdrawing more and more from the world each year. Or, third, we allow our pain to transform us into beings of infinite compassion. Knowing what it's like to feel the sting of being alive, we can't help but feel empathy for all others and never desire to be the cause of another person's suffering. When the third outcome is cultivated in full, it's very similar in nature to the joyful sadness experienced in the Galactic Consciousness. Because of life, we feel pain and sadness, and because of life, we also feel joy and gratitude.

No-thing can satisfy our thirst, yet we can eliminate the thirst by releasing our attachments to the mundane world.

As I shared in my flashback story, I was able to find happiness and peace despite the great physical pain I was in, the extreme weight of financial burdens, and living in a construction zone. Although there are many who live in far more extreme conditions around the world, the average American can relate to my story. In fact, statistics show that remodeling homes causes great relationship and family strain, divorce, depression, and even suicide. When our nest is disturbed, it easily creates imbalance in every area of our life. This is why Release the Mundane is such a powerful teaching. It helps us recognize the true value of life, rather than the glittering, superficial things we often chase and attempt to build our lives upon.

Please remember: The most important things in life aren't

tangible!

Ever since I was a child, I admired monks, especially eastern monks who always seemed so peaceful and somehow jovial in nature. As I grew older, I found out how some — like the Dalai Lama and Thich Nhat Hanh — had experienced war in their countries, watched as their people were killed, and then were exiled, banned from ever returning to their homelands. In Thich Nhat Hanh's case, he was exiled for peacefully protesting the Vietnam War. These monks, like many others, serve as an incredible source of inspiration when coming to understand that even when one loses everything — inner peace is still possible.

What are your complaints? What are your gripes? In politics and religion throughout the world, there still is much finger-pointing and aggression towards anyone who is "different" and thereby challenges what we deem familiar, safe, and comfortable. We saw this at its height during World War II with Hitler's persecution of the Jewish people. Today, an ever-increasing, world-wide, collective intolerance continues. People are electing and following leaders who show zero kindness, compassion, or empathy for anyone outside their familiar bubble. The result of this kind of mentality can never be peace, yet we repeatedly forget this as a species, instead choosing leaders promote a false sense of comfort and security while granting us permission to remain in the Mundane & Collective layers of consciousness, which validate our egoic judgments and fears.

I share all of this because, if we are not mindful enough, our attachments to the Mundane will plunge us into a deep sleep, with intolerance and fear directing our dreams until they eventually become waking nightmares in our society. We say that this isn't possible, yet history has been known to repeat itself time and again for people who are not mindful of it.

Our call to action in this tenet is to begin applying its wisdom throughout our daily lives and within our very homes. As we will soon cover in the practice portion of this chapter, we are invited to cultivate attitudes of gratitude each day to counterbalance our complaints, fears, and attachments to nonessentials. How we choose to live our daily lives and what we choose to focus on has more power than most realize, trapping the mind in years of suffering if we aren't careful. It is important to realize and embrace that our ordinary life *is* our spiritual life; there is no separation between the two.

Practice 7
Counting Gratitudes
(*Release the Mundane*)

This practice of counting gratitudes can be done immediately and consistently. Whether you are alone, in a relationship, or perhaps a single parent, this practice can be altered to fit any situation, and it has tremendous benefit. Every night, just before bed, recount your gratitudes out loud for every person, place, or thing you are thankful for. If married, when one partner goes to bed, the other is invited to join in for this present-moment activation of gratitude.

Most do not do this. Ego gets in the way and pulls the focus of the mind to more things to complain or worry about. For couples, it may also be uncomfortable, or even scary, to share these moments of gratitude because this kind of mental and emotionally vulnerable intimacy, with undivided attention, has been lost between the two, or possibly it never even existed. However, this strengthening of heart-to-heart connection is just another reason to do this practice!

Parents, please also share this practice with your child (or children). Even if just one gratitude per night is shared followed by a goodnight kiss and an, "I love you" — this simple practice is beyond priceless in terms of cultivating loving communication and presence-giving, both of which are challenges many adults struggle with, especially when single and trying to provide the basics. Learning these practices young is exceptionally worthwhile!

If you live alone or have no one to consistently call to share your gratitudes with, keeping a gratitude journal is another powerful way of activating the wonderful vibrations and perspectives that come with this practice. Don't be afraid to talk to yourself, write to yourself, or communicate with whatever God or Being you may believe in. Additionally, you may choose to talk to a loved one who has crossed over. There is no "wrong" way to do this practice, the primary purpose being simply for you to call to mind moments, interactions, things, and people throughout your day that you can be grateful for.

About six months into our relationship, my now-husband, Andrew, encouraged this nightly ritual of counting gratitudes. To this day, we haven't missed a night, and we have no intention of ever stopping this practice!

Truthfully, there were a few times after our move to Colorado, during the difficult process of remodeling our new home and business, that I found myself so exhausted I couldn't summon any sense of gratitude. Even though I did not feel grateful, I still showed up to do this practice with Andrew and thanked our challenges for helping me grow (albeit through pain). On those nights, this practice didn't make me feel better, but feeling better wasn't the point. The point was to maintain our practice of looking beyond the surface-level pains of the Mundane Consciousness and the temporary discomforts of our physical, earthly (mundane) reality. By doing so, I expanded my mind's awareness to share gratitudes outside our little bubble of temporary discomfort, thanking and blessing the people in my life, past and present. As you can see, it's possible — and important — to maintain this practice even when life exhausts us or we're in a not-so-happy mood.

An additional spin-off practice you may choose that also cultivates the mindset of gratitude is the Practice of Limitation. Counting Gratitudes is an everyday practice. The Practice of Limitation can be done once a month or a few times each year depending on your preference. The purpose of this expanded practice is to give up something of comfort to help us acknowledge our attachments and realize that we don't need them to be happy. Additionally, giving up a comfort or a soft addiction (such as a favorite food, form of entertainment, or physical pleasure) is likely to reveal resistances or irritations that were hidden. This practice is another wonderful way to help us deepen our recognition of the parts of our ego and subconscious mind that can still use some gentle tending to!

Tenet Eight:
Release Knowing

Flashback:

A huge issue I had for many years was the need to "know", to understand, and to solve problems each time knots in my relationships manifested. I was an extreme people-pleaser and analyzer, so as soon as anything felt "off" in my close ties, I felt I had to fix it. This was a major drain on me – and if I'm being fully honest here – it was also selfish. Often, the relationships that fell from my life weren't in my best interest, anyway, yet I couldn't stand feeling someone was upset with me and not knowing why. Thus, I'd often wriggle myself back into a connection that was long overdue to be released.

One year, I decided to stop trying to fix and save every delicate "vase" that broke in my life. I was done spending so much wasted time trying to patch up the shards of each person's un-communicated feelings. I made a personal vow and told the people closest to me of my new intention for friendship. Since my work life involved helping people solve their emotional problems, it wasn't healthy to have as friends people whose emotions I also had to constantly worry about. Exhausted from always being "on", I was ready for friends I didn't have to walk on eggshells around who accepted me inherently for me and told me the truth no matter what.

During the year I had my friendship "revelation", a couple of close friends did leave my life, but a few other friendships strengthened exponentially. It was a risk I had to take, a loss I had to bear in order to get to where I am today. My inner circle of friendship is now one of complete transparency, respect, kindness, and unconditional love. But first, I had to embody what I sought by being honest and direct with everyone in my life, even if it hurt.

An example was when I felt it might have been time to release a close friend who'd been continuously unsupportive. Our friendship had begun in my adolescence, so he was someone I had a sentimental fondness for and a genuine acceptance of. To practice what I preached – rather than avoiding an uncomfortable conversation and making the choice for him, assuming he wouldn't be receptive – I took him to lunch and vulnerably spoke from the heart. I expressed that I felt a sad hesitancy to invite him to my upcoming wedding because, for the past year, he'd shown no happiness for me in my new relationship or any interest to meet my soon-to-be husband.

To my surprise, my friend took the news very well. Although it still hurt, he said something was indeed "off" for me to express this, and he opened up about his own struggles with depression and self-worth during the past year. He genuinely didn't want to hurt or push me away with his moods, so this was a great awareness for him to hear. He later said it inspired him to seek and follow through with professional help to change his life for the better.

The transparent conversation I had with my friend promoted a powerful bonding and healing between us – and he did come to the wedding. Near or far, he's a friend I'll always cherish, and now I know that I can be fully authentic and honest with him, no matter how difficult or painful. This kind of friendship is priceless – no masks or assumptions, just truth.

Had I not practiced the wisdom of this tenet in releasing my assumptions, I would never have approached my friend with full honesty and potentially could have lost a loving friendship.

≫ ≫ ≫ ≪ ≪ ≪

It's so important to not get caught up in the ego belief of "I Know". Once we attach to "knowing", it limits our ability to continue learning and begin to see the bigger picture of life through the Layers of Consciousness. "Knowing" is one of the biggest obstacles my students have to overcome. They get to a point of believing that they've worked hard enough and have learned enough that they no longer need their daily practices to maintain balance. The more their egos puff them up with the illusion of "knowing", the less able they are to learn and relearn. They grow bored, become more easily frustrated, and blame others for their discontinued learning. They may also become self-righteous in *telling* people what they "know". It's hard to fill a cup that's — supposedly — already full. Often, the student will fall "asleep" again when they get caught back up in the Mundane Consciousness. Since they are no longer doing their daily practice to ground and center themselves, ego takes over, and with a growing attitude of self-righteous indignation, they begin pointing fingers once more, ignoring the reflection of themselves that's mirrored in the world around them. Spiritual arrogance and pride is a dangerous rabbit hole to fall down. Humility and vulnerability are the tools necessary to keep us out.

We are not in these human forms to project our reality onto other people. We are not here to try to change other people's colors and behaviors to match our own. We are here to marvel at the diversity of life, creating our reality to fit our highest desires while giving others the same freedom. Once we understand and accept that we do not "know" what's best for anyone else, we can move on to releasing other forms of attachment "knowing" also manifests as.

We must also always remember that the consistency of our practice maintains our vibrational reality of peace — not the achievement of learning or "knowing". **Enlightenment is about "being", not "knowing"**. In order to **"be"** we **"do"** what allows us to embody the illuminated lifestyle that eventually brings enlightenment and inner peace. And so, we do our work, and we do it well. Each morning is a new day in which all that exists is the present moment — a brand new moment. We embrace all our teachings, interactions, and experiences with a student's mind — the mind of a beginner.

Let's clarify "doing": We, as perpetual students, move toward enlightenment, consistently doing the work. I often express to my students that all the Master Teachers of the world maintain their embodiment of peace and enlightened state of "being" by living and breathing the lifestyle. Whatever background they come from, their physical and spiritual practices reflect their commitment to their path. Some meditate at length daily; train their bodies; fast and cleanse; pray and chant; create music, poetry, or art; continue to study and hone their minds; provide selfless service, and so on.

Master Teachers who genuinely embody an enlightened state of being never stop "doing the work". The ego is what assumes it "knows" enough, causing the cessation of these daily practices. Therefore, Masters without ego attachment are forever students of the Universe. These Masters attain an illuminated state of "Being" as their outcome, yet it is the consistent "doing" that promotes and maintains their enlightenment. After all, our ordinary life *is* our spiritual life—there is no separation between the two.

Taking the concept a step further in an esoteric light—all that exists is the present moment. That means every new day is a **completely** NEW day. Thus, what we learned yesterday is gone—until we activate it in our minds and vibrational auras today, in the NOW. The ritual of daily practice is crucial because it honors the impermanent nature of life. Whatever we do not perceive, think, feel, or do might as well not exist in our present moment reality. In fact, it DOES NOT exist in our present moment reality. And so, bringing the necessary practice into the present moment each day via our mental awareness is what creates a reality of *Living Peace*.

≫ ≫ ≫ ≪ ≪ ≪

I always taught my students that we never "know" what's best for another individual even as teachers, yet it wasn't until I put myself in the role of a student in Aikido that I learned the full meaning of this insight.

During the first few months of my Aikido experience, I often felt pressured by my Sensei (teacher) and his projections and expectations about what I needed to learn. His attitude amused me to some degree, since he often dropped passive-aggressive hints in class that I, of course, picked up on. He wanted to foster the best in me, and I appreciated his feedback and gentle nudges to grow. However, the number one projection was his opinion that I wasn't committed enough. In his mind, it was an accurate observation, but, for my desired goals, I was as committed as I needed to be and was getting everything I ever wanted to out of the class.

When I took a hiatus, I expressed my perspective and gratitude for the training we completed and shared that I felt completely fulfilled, having received what I joined the class for. He had an enlightened moment, for his response to me was, "I have learned something from this, as well. Everyone comes to Aikido for their own reasons. And as long as they are getting what they need from their commitment, then I need to let them be, instead of driving them towards my idea of what I want for them. So, thank you for bringing that to my awareness."

We teachers, parents, leaders, and role models do act as guides for others as they travel their chosen paths. In my own teaching, I balance what my students desire to learn with growth opportunities, areas of possible benefit that they may not think of for themselves.

The week following the experience with my Sensei, I went to a student of mine and told her I hoped she didn't feel pressured by me to take her progression test before she felt ready. I assured her I was there to help her in any way she needed. She expressed that she was receiving everything she ever wanted out of my class and didn't necessarily feel the need to progress further at that particular moment. She reflected the same feelings I'd expressed during the same kind of talk with my Sensei. What a truly marvelous mirror experience!

The concept of humility is an important one as we move forward along this journey. True humility is accepting one's self through and through and not needing validation from anyone else to feel secure. An excellent instance of humility is a friend of mine who's a doctor, yet he never calls attention to that fact. He began attending Sunday services, and for the longest time no one knew about his occupation. He has a quiet humbleness about him that allows him to simply be present in his illumination. He doesn't need people to view him a certain way based on a Mundane attachment to identity and achievement.

This is in stark contrast to another dear friend who'd previously attended and made sure everyone knew her Ph.D. status and called her by the correct title. Please realize, I'm not saying never to use titles — the question we must ask ourselves is whether or not we're attached to their accomplishment as part of our identities.

Some of us have the burning desire to tell the world who we are, rather than let it naturally be discovered in time. There are great attachments to "having to know" or "having to be known" and all of them are illusions. No one will ever "know" us through and through, because the moment they meet us, they subconsciously observe, analyze and decide on an aspect that matches their vibration, and that's who they see us as. Who we are in other people's minds has more to do with them than it does us.

The same thing occurs when we meet, observe and analyze other people, situations, and life as a whole. Our opinion about them is more a reflection of us than it is them. Everything that's perceived in life by an individual is a projection of their vibrational aura — or rather, their collective thoughts, emotions, and past experiences that led to a biased filter through which they now perceive the world.

Understanding people's biased projections lets us off the hook of trying to figure everyone and everything out, so we can cease trying to please the world. We can release the need to "know" and start showing up in life worry free. In truth, that's all we ever can do. We are then able to be more authentically free and vulnerable.

Vulnerability means being strong and secure enough in yourself that you can walk outside without your armor on. You are able to fully show up in life, no matter the situation, and just be you. Living with the openness and tenderness of vulnerability takes genuine strength and courage. Armor may look tough, but all it does is mask insecurity and fear.

There is such power in vulnerability. In many people's eyes, vulnerability is a weakness, yet there's actually nothing more courageous than showing up in the world and being authentically you! In a culture dominated by superficiality and insecurity, we always find it a breath of fresh air whenever we see someone openly being themselves. As the marvelous saying goes, "What other people think about me is none of my business!"

"What is being authentic?" some may ask. "Authenticity" is a word that's thrown around a lot, so to clarify, it means the ability to be fully honest and sincere at all times — not wearing any masks or hiding thoughts or feelings due to insecurity.

Another aspect of being vulnerable is venturing into the unknown. People often stay in a painful situation rather than try something new because it's what they're used to. At least it's familiar, and an unknown outcome is not. **Some might**

think that a person who allows him or herself to be abused is someone who is also vulnerable. The opposite is true — they are being abused because they're not willing to be vulnerable. Vulnerability takes strength and courage. Part of being vulnerable includes saying, "I'm comfortable enough in my own skin, and I trust in my ability to leave this abusive relationship. Even though I fear being alone, and I fear the unknown, I'd rather be alone in the unknown than stay in this toxic relationship that is b-eating me alive." Having worked with many people who've suffered because of abusive relationships, the idea of vulnerability being courageous is something that's produced a universal "ah-ha" moment for many of my clients and students, past and present.

Vulnerability is built on the last chapter's Release the Mundane. In releasing our attachment to the Mundane world we develop trust in ourselves and our own capabilities. In next releasing our attachment to "knowing", we develop the strength and courage of vulnerability. We realize more and more that there's no controlling anything or anyone outside ourselves, and we accept, more and more, reality as it is. When we accept reality as is, we cease resisting it or trying to change it. Instead, we look within for the answers and begin to take steps that benefit our lives for the highest good rather than compromising ourselves out of fear, or denial, insisting things will change for the better even though we're taking no action to create that change.

≫ ≫ ≫ ≪ ≪ ≪

This is crucial to read again:

It is important to not get caught up in the ego of "I Know." Once we attach to the belief of "knowing" something or someone, it limits our ability to continue learning and being able to see the bigger picture of life through the Layers of Consciousness.

The more our ego puffs us up with the illusion of "knowing", the less we're able to learn. It's hard to fill a cup that's — supposedly — already full. We must always remember that it is the consistency of our practice that maintains our vibrational reality of peace — not the achievements of learning or "knowing".

Enlightenment is about "being" — not knowing. **To "be" is to "do".**

If we're not actively doing what we've learned and still causing dramas and messes for ourselves, then we can be assured that we <u>do not "know"</u>, for if we did, we wouldn't be recreating and reinforcing old patterns of pain.

Concluding Thoughts

A daily practice of mine to is look at the world through fresh eyes each morning. It's a brand new day with new experiences to be had, and so I go forth with the wonder and joy of a child who's eager to explore. When meditating and doing my centering practices, I use my student's mind — always ready to improve and to learn more. When I read inspired words of wisdom, I read them as if it's the first time, even if I've read them a thousand times before. Every day is a new day, and every NOW moment is all that exists — both past and future are illusion. In each NOW moment, I am born anew, and I look at the world through new eyes and experience everything for the first time. I am forever a student of the Universe, and my heart and mind are ever expanding.

It's an interesting conundrum when it comes to "Knowing." On one hand, we're told to "know" ourselves. On the other hand we're told to "release all knowing". The way I understand and practically apply this seeming contradiction is by internally developing a "knowing" relationship with myself, while externally always releasing my judgments, opinions, expectations, and attachments to "knowing" the world and its people. What's beautiful to also understand is that we are always in a state of **Be**coming. We can "know" plenty about ourselves, yet we will never fully KNOW ourselves since each new day brings new experiences and realizations that further our perpetual state of **Be**coming.

Practice 8
Mask Removal
(Release Knowing)

Mask Removal taps into the reality that when we are fully authentic, we're the same person in any crowd. Unfortunately, it's the commonly accepted norm to don different masks and act in different ways depending on the people we're with. Some fluctuation is normal, yet what often occurs is the suppression of self through fear of judgment or compassionately not wanting to create unnecessary waves by making the people we love feel uncomfortable. For instance, children and grandchildren grow up and frequently become someone very different from the innocent, compliant kid their parents or grandparents perceived them to be when they gain their "freedom".

Let's recap "being authentic". Embracing authenticity is the ability to be fully honest and sincere at all times — not wearing any masks or hiding our inner thoughts or feelings due to insecurity.

There are two beliefs and practices I will share next. The first is **there is no suppression in unconditional love or peace.** It can be very uncomfortable to fully share one's differing religious or political ideologies, to come out of the gender or sexual-orientation closet, or to choose not to follow certain cultural traditions — such as marrying or participating in other rites of passage. The weight of disappointing those we love often keeps us stuck, continuing to wear masks, which can slowly drain our spirit and obliterate our happiness. This first approach to Mask Removal invites us to be honest, even when it hurts. Please note that this honesty doesn't involve getting into arguments or losing our emotional balance. If you can't maintain your peace during these difficult conversations it may be of benefit to wait momentarily until you can. Key: *momentarily* — don't use your wavering emotions as an escape route so that you never have to address the hard topics! Seek training then face your discomfort and fears by removing your masks.

The importance of this first approach is that it challenges comfort zones, belief systems, and shatters delusions that others have about us (images of who we are to them that they cling to out of attachment). The result of our full honesty is that it gives others a chance to love us for who we really are — not just who they *think* we are. It helps make the world a more loving, accepting, and understanding place.

This topic hits close to home for me because, I came out of the closet as a teen, which was a very scary thing to do at the time. My whole perceived identity changed when everyone stopped holding me to the unfair standard of being a "straight boy or man". Taking off the mask of my sexuality was freeing and helped lift my depression. Since then, I've helped numerous others come out of the closet, all of whom have ultimately lived happier lives, though at first some received negative pushback from certain loved ones.

The second approach to Mask Removal is a unique one in that it asks us to jump ahead to Releasing Self. (Once you've fully read the last tenet, this will make more sense.) When we Release Self, we have little concern about our personal identity, and although we won't ever lie or withhold truth, it's much easier to participate in our loved ones' traditions and beliefs, even if they don't match our own. An excellent example: choosing to engage in a specific wedding ceremony or ritual that's of major importance to our parents. It may not mean much to us, yet to them it means the world. We could fight over this, or we can choose to do what speaks to our hearts but also provide our parents with what brings their hearts happiness.

Creating conflicts for the sake of standing our ground by forcing others to accept us and our differing choices is not the way of peace. When we Release Self, we naturally un-attach from this tug-of-war because we no longer feel offended or threatened by anyone. When we come home for holidays, we can visit our family's favorite church. If we visit people of a different culture who express their friendship and hospitality via food, we eat what's offered even if it's something we don't prefer. Some may also invite us to wear certain clothing, and we do so without hesitation, even if it makes no sense or seems suppressing to us.

We can now remove the mask of our own identity to show up for others more fully, building bridges over our differences through kind interactions within their experienced realities. If we stick too firmly to personal identity, many of these bridges might not ever be built because we're too unwilling to step outside our comfort zone or relax our religious-political-personal stances.

As you can see, there is no perfect path when it comes to Mask Removal. On one hand, we initiate the difficult conversations that encourage growth, even if that growth comes through pain and shattered illusions. On the other hand, we become so skilled at Releasing Self that we don't mind temporarily assuming a role that makes our loved ones happy or allows us to step into the diverse realities of other cultures all over the world. The middle ground balances never telling lies with forever being kind. This is actively "doing" rather than only "knowing", making Mask Removal a powerful practice to bring into your life.

The Practice

The practice of Mask Removal can also be applied in our daily lives by consciously choosing to never tell white lies and eventually divulging all big secrets we still keep. This may take the form of telling the truth about an affair, past or present, difficult past traumas experienced, hidden addictions, even honest feelings about how you may be struggling in your marriage, or with being a parent, caregiver, breadwinner, etc. Whether your secrets are big or are the subtler emotional hardships of living that you don't want others to see, removing all masks through honesty often strengthens relationships and provides opportunities for genuine understanding between partners and among people in general. Others can sense our dissatisfaction or hiddenness, especially since our heaviness often leads to distancing and behaving irritability. When we pierce the wall of separation by telling the full truth, it usually leads to relief because those around us can finally begin to understand why something was "off" and accept us better. Always remember: **we cannot heal what we do not acknowledge.**

Finally, many of us fear taking off our masks — not because we're afraid of hurting others or ourselves — but because we're ultimately afraid of change, specifically of having to change. If we removed certain masks, our world might quickly begin to change, and this terrifies us. We've grown accustomed to our familiar life, so we think it's easier to just keep playing along, even if we're miserable. A word of wisdom regarding this dilemma: Things won't ever get easier, and there won't ever be a perfect time to shatter an illusion. However, the sooner we do tell the full truth and remove all masks, the sooner we can pick up the pieces and begin living an authentic life of our own making.

Give others the chance to love you for *you*. You may be surprised with the outcome! Even if things don't go smoothly at first, at least now others will begin to see that you're authentically open. Soon, people will come into your life because they match your new vibration and your authentic being. Don't be afraid of the quiet gap that exists between your old life and the new one. This "gap period" is always temporary and is actually a time of pure potential!

Tenet Nine:

Release Self

Flashback:

Note: It took me four years since writing this book to begin embodying this tenet's wisdom consistently. This length of time is actually quite normal since Release Self is the most difficult tenet to fully apply because it calls for us to bring together and integrate everything we've learned up to this point.

I opened Earth Spirit Center for Healing in the late summer of 2010 when I was twenty years old, and yes, I was pretty much just a kid playing at business with my best friend, whom I hired as my secretary. For the first year, it was fun, but I didn't do much or make much money until I started collaborating with others. I began facilitating monthly Public Healing Nights, and at their peak, this brought in nearly a hundred people. Due to what I gained from these Healing Nights, my little business eventually evolved into a successful center, including a consistent community that became the foundation upon which I founded Earth Spirit Church.

I had a knack for bringing people together, and my happy-go-lucky, innocent nature inspired many folks to join. However, due to my own lack of experience and naivety, I leaned more on other people's judgment instead of relying on my own inner guidance. This led to personal boundary issues, and, eventually, the co-dependency of seeking approval from others.

As the leader of this spontaneously established community of a few dozen committed members (and several dozen more loosely associated people), I had a lot of responsibilities to juggle all at once. Soon, the issues that all too often plague other churches began to arise: power struggles, gossip, and behind-the-scenes drama. These issues eventually consumed me. Every week, it seemed my job as peacemaker expanded exponentially. Instead of having time to actually enjoy my life and grow the church, I grew exhausted from constantly putting out fires between members. Over time, the twinkle in my eyes vanished and I began to numb myself, going through the motions with a smile tacked on my face so no one would see the truth of my unhappiness.

After two years of being a selfless pastor (literally self-less: all my blood, sweat, tears, time, and money), I decided to step down as pastor, and the church eventually dissolved. I made no money during the two years of the church's existence since most of my services and sermons had been given freely without requiring tithes, and the small amount of money we did bring in from offerings went back into keeping the church alive and the center running. Earth Spirit Church was a success among the people, touching hundreds of lives in that short amount of time, but without regular tithing it couldn't survive. In those days, I honestly did feel "bad" when asking for money. Now, I understand the vital importance of equal energy exchange.

Years later, as I write this revised edition, I find myself once again leading a community and starting another church. What I've come to realize since my last stint as pastor is that Release Self isn't the same as being self-less. In my younger years, I simply didn't "know" my Self. I didn't know my boundaries, my strength, or my ability to truly lead. I didn't know the depths of my own empathy and compassion, or the depths of my own ego and pain. The irony is that in order to truly release one's Self, one must know him Self or her Self through and through. I can now step out of "my" own way any time I find emotional attachment occurring, while also standing firm in my resolve of peace whenever conflict arises. Long lasting and effective leadership cannot occur without great depths of self-awareness that is followed by the eventual Releasing of Self.

A telltale sign of mastering Release Self is the state of being perpetually relaxed, a state achieved when we no longer feel threatened by others or the happenings of Life. We no longer function in a fight or flight mode. Instead, we are able to be fully present and at peace within ourselves no matter what the external circumstance. To the untrained eye, this behavior may seem aloof or naive, yet the ability to remain perpetually relaxed means we have mastered some of the world's deepest wisdom. Once we Release Self, our body and mind can relax because we understand and accept life's impermanence. We do our work and we do it well--without worry, struggle, or resistance. We improve what we can and help where we can, and everything else we have no control over we let go, understanding that any thoughts or emotion spent on what's out of our hands is wasted energy.

When we are led by ego's delusion, many of us try to create solid ground in mentally created landscapes. Examples of this are: regretting the past or feeling anxious about the future, worrying about the opinions of others or fearing change in any of its forms. Although we can learn from the past and plan for the future, we need not be consumed or emotionally charged by them. We learn and plan from a place of relaxed (peaceful) awareness and action.

You cannot become offended if you have no identified Self.

"Self" defined: the perceived and believed sense of identity (external) and personality (internal). Identity relates to the external characteristics that the world sees, such as our appearance, gender, accomplishments, Dis-Eases, and religious and political affiliations. Personality relates to our likes and dislikes, general demeanor, and collective emotional expression. Although these two aspects that make up our Self exist and influence our lives, our goal is to release our attachment to them with the understanding that we are much more than our perceived identity and perceived personality.

So much of our world's aggressive and defensiveness occurs when people, as individuals or groups, take offense to things. In my early twenties, during the time I was an interfaith pastor, I started a Sunday sermon by giving my congregation the middle finger and saying, "Fuck You!" in a serious tone. Some laughed, some were confused or uncomfortable, while others noticed an irritation rise within them from the gesture. Then I blatantly said, "If you were triggered by this in any way — we have work to do!" The purpose of my exercise was to show people that any offense taken is purely psychological, and therefore is illusion of our own making when we label certain things or actions dualistically. We know this to be true because, depending on one's culture, these words and gestures have completely different meanings!

Why do we have an emotional response when other people flip us off? It's because our "Self" feels threatened or bothered by it. But if we Release our Self, what then? We remain neutral and relaxed, thus gaining the ability to more effectively respond to the situation, or any situation, for that matter.

"No longer a woman"

Another example of Release Self that I gave one of my students as homework was to release identifying as a woman. She was a strong, older woman who grew up fighting tooth and nail to get her piece of pie when America was predominantly male-focused, especially in the work force. As a single mom, she raised her son, put herself through college, and became a nurse practitioner. Her story is very inspiring! Yet, years later, she still harbored resentment over the way our society continues to perpetuate the male-female divide. It often amused me how, in nearly every session, she skillfully tied her identity as a woman into the conversation by making a comment or rant about how hard it was, and sometimes still is.

One day, I pointed this pattern out to her and gave her the homework to "release being a woman" for a couple weeks, just to see what might happen. When she came back, her entire demeanor had changed and she was so much more relaxed! We both concluded that this releasing didn't negate her hardship, or the continued hardship of all women around the world — what it did was help her maintain her peace and stop identifying with her Self and collected experiences. Now, she can describe the struggles of female inequality from a place of peace and precise communication, whereas before her fiery rants may have caused the people she was trying to reach to tune her out.

Note: I had to do this very same practice, releasing my identity of being a gay man and the many past (and present) struggles with societal prejudice.

We are more than our perceived past and more than our perceived present. Although it's important to identify inequality, inequality exists because we become overly attached to this temporary shell of a body we reside in, to our birthplace, to our accomplishments and gains, as well as to our mental attachments (beliefs and opinions). We are just so **sure** of ourselves and so **sure** of the world that this certainty can cause ourselves and others tremendous suffering due to self-righteousness or self-pity. There's a lot of power in removing "Self" from the equation of our lives, and when we do, we begin to see life clearly for the first time — as pure observers without bias, prejudice, emotional filters, or fears.

Please always remember:
You do not have to be defined by who you think you are, or the life you've lived up to this point.

≫ ≫ ≫ ≪ ≪ ≪

The paradox of self-actualization and release

As mentioned in the flashback story, "we must know

ourselves before we can release ourselves" — which may seem a bit paradoxical since the previous tenet was Release Knowing. The first seven tenets were about learning to understand ourselves, and the eighth was about releasing said knowing (otherwise self-inflated duality/ego creeps back in), so we can fully step into the final tenet of Release Self. Each tenet beautifully builds on top of the previous one, creating a stable foundation and structure in which we may achieve inner peace and expanding states of consciousness. And yet, Release Self reminds us that this journey is not about "us" — nor has it ever been.

We start the *Inner Peace* journey under the delusional goal of achieving inner peace for our own relief and wellbeing, or for enlightenment. However, when we finally get to the end (never truly the end), our delusion of separation is shattered. We realize that our lives are but a collection of droplets in a cosmic ocean — or, for the spiritually-minded, we are a gathering of souls that make up the Universe. The ocean cannot exist without each droplet, just as we cannot exist without each other. Everything and everyone is interconnected. Previously we believed we were all separate, yet it is our combined consciousness that creates the world we see and enjoy (or suffer from). It's our choice to create and recreate what we experience through our six senses, and now, we have the tools to alleviate not only our own suffering, but the collective suffering of those on our planet through first embodying peace and then teaching peace.

When people try to help the world without first Releasing Self, their assistance is often riddled with selfishness and egocentric thinking. Over-sympathizing is often connected with feeling pity or "bad" for the "less fortunate". Without our new awareness, we slip into the well-meaning judgments of the savior complex. Sometimes, our motivation to help may even arise out of feelings of discomfort or guilt. By "helping" we feel gratified and pat ourselves on the back for a "job well done" and being a "good person" who gives back — only to return to our Mundane dramas and personal bubbles, completely forgetting about the rest of the world and its problems until next time.

*A very common "unhelpful helping" takes place every day in many relationships and marriages. We hear our loved ones complaining about something, and, in "feeling bad" for them, we immediately chime in with solutions. Shortly thereafter our loved one reacts by saying, "you're not listening" or "you don't understand". Because we're well-meaning – just trying to help – we feel lost and confused. We act on what **we** think is in their best interest instead of taking the time to step out of our own opinions and ask what **they** need in the moment or what they would like help with later on. Practicing this kind of communication allows us to see the world not just through our eyes, but through the eyes of the people we care about and are trying to assist.*

Release Self allows us to "break the mirror" so we no longer see reflections of ourselves in everyone. Instead, we begin to see each individual as an individual — without comparisons and biases to cloud our vision. In this way, we gain the ability to see life through the eyes of others and cease trying to change or create the world in our own image. This unconditional freedom is the very nature of love, what some may even call divine.

Unconditional Love

Unconditional love becomes possible when we have inner peace because unconditional love *is* the outward expression of inner peace. Please always remember that love clouded by attachment often leads to unloving behavior and emotional unrest, while love coming from the clear place of our inner peace allows for kindness, patience, respect, and offering help without agenda. We've likely all heard the saying, "You can't love anyone else until you love yourself." What this means is: as long as we abuse ourselves, we will allow others to abuse us in equal measure or spill our self-abuse and criticism onto those closest to us. This wisdom shows us the dire importance of cultivating a peaceful heart, mind, and spirit — which leads us to the final teaching of Resurgence.

Resurgence

As we come to the close of this tenet and our study of the Living Peace Code, a Resurgence occurs, which is the revival of Mastery of Thought. We now cycle around and start anew at the beginning of this book and its teachings. The ultimate wisdom of *Living Peace* and also of living, is that we never fully "finish", and we can never get it wrong. Life is a continuum, much like these nine teachings that help us become more awake, aware, and alive to our journey through this human experience.

You are now invited to go back to the beginning, to your innocence, and read through this book again with fresh eyes and a beginner's mind. Practice every teaching as if for the first time, never becoming bored or inflated with "knowing". The true-Truth is that every day is in fact a new day, so what you learned yesterday no longer exists until you invoke it in the present moment.

As you continue your practice, walking this lifestyle of peace, you will undoubtedly notice its calming effect. Wisdom is cool and collected, never explosive or aggressive. Resurgence keeps you watered with wisdom's cooling, nourishing rains. Each raindrop is a thought, a word, a smile, an act of kindness, a moment in meditation. Nurture yourself, others, and the land, as you apply each of the nine tenets in unison throughout your entire life, each and every day

Practice 9
The Deliberate Choice of Peace
(*Release Self*)

At the end of the day, the Living Peace Code teachings come down to one thing: Are you going to choose to walk this path, or not?

Are you going to meet the challenges that occur with peace? Are you going to rise above them? Are you going to hone your practices daily? Or are you going to read this book, compliment it for containing nice words and ideals, and then go back to your former life, forgetting the majority of what was shared in these pages?

I've met thousands of spiritual practitioners and teachers who idealize saints and gurus, yet when it really matters, the majority of them don't practice what they preach. When the going gets tough, "negative" thoughts take over, impulses run rampant, and their emotions get the better of them. They get lost in Illusion, where duality holds powerful sway, and within the duality lies chaos and ignorance. And when chaos and ignorance hold sway, there is such fear, such fear, of not having enough, such fear of being fully seen and vulnerable, such fear of really looking themselves in the mirror and facing the Self behind their reflections. Instead of rising to the challenge and answering the call, most decide to go back to sleep because it's easier that way. And it's okay if they do — there is no judgment, and there is no right or wrong way to live.

To those who do want to follow this path, or at least apply some of the *Living Peace* teachings to their lives, there's one thing left for me to really drive home. **You must do the work.**

It's not enough to "know" what the work is or to talk about it. Knowledge means nothing and holds no power until it is applied and used. You must make the deliberate choice to choose peace, day in and day out. Make it a conscious way of living with every breath you take. When peace resides in the forefront of your mind on a daily basis, it will forever be the lens through which you filter all your thoughts, emotions and actions.

The Practice

This practice is quite literally the simplest, yet the most difficult to fully master and apply. The practice is to choose peace in every area of your life: every conversation, every conflict, every work and social interaction. Every prayer, meditation, energy exchange, every laugh and smile. Every thought, emotion, impulse, word, and action. Imbue peace into the beliefs in your subconscious mind.

How do we do this? We do this by reading this book — or any peace teaching that resonates — again and again, applying the practices on a daily basis and developing consistency of character. We do so until we masterfully embody peace, and when we masterfully embody peace, we realize we will forever continue to keep up our practices and begin to teach and share them with others.

I've been given the excuse of, "I'm human; complete peace is impossible."

This belief is pure illusion. It's because we *are* human that we *are* capable of creating lives and realities of peace. And it is because we *are* human that it's so very possible for world peace to become reality. Humans are gifted with free will and the divine ability to influence and create reality. It is this free will and this ability to create that allows us to do just that! We can make this planet a living and thriving paradise if we but choose it!

Some then say that it's impossible, that because of free will, we can't get everyone to agree or to all want the same thing. However, peace does not demand that everyone like or want the same reality. Peace gives each individual the freedom to create their best life, while that individual gives the same respect and freedom to their neighbor. This is where we've slipped up. In the past, our idea of peace has been conformity. Yet the only way for world peace to exist is through a mutual respect that honors diversity and realizes all the beauty and freedom that individuality brings.

There is one thing that humanity can agree on: that peace, joy, and love offer the highest vibration for humans to dwell and thrive in.

The Vow

Every day, consciously and deliberately, I reaffirm my vow of *Living Peace*.

The Cosmic Ocean

Each of us is an individual soul that, when joined together with other souls, forms the Universe just as each droplet of water forms the ocean. One does not exist without the other, and just as all water eventually finds its way back to the ocean, so do all souls find their way back to the Cosmic Consciousness.

Why we are here...

Imagine if each droplet of water became crystal clear and purified, free of all pollution and taint; what would happen to the ocean? As a whole, it would reflect that purity and be crystal clear. The same applies to each soul affecting the Universe. When we each raise our vibrations to higher levels of consciousness through embodying peace and expanding our awareness, the reflection expands and elevates the Universe.

We are here to learn, grow, expand, transcend, and ascend. There is no duality of "good" or "bad", "right" or "wrong", "dark" against "light", or even self against any other. Duality is a manmade concept, and, as long as we hold onto this fabricated notion, we will forever be trapped by it, continuously perpetuating separation and causing unnecessary rifts in humanity.

These rifts begin in the home and expand outward to become the crux of every war. If we can find peace within our hearts, the massive conflicts that have been repeated throughout history will not continue to be perpetrated. While still in these physical bodies, **we are evolving from Homo-sapiens to Homo-luminous** — a consciousness and spiritual evolution. We no longer need be trapped by our egos or the karma of what once was, forever to repeat and never to transcend. We can start learning and growing through the conscious choice of peace and joy rather than suffering. It is true that the deeper the hurt, the greater the opportunity we have to learn from it, yet we are now coming upon an era in which we will choose to learn and consciously expand more swiftly due to a foundation of peace.

Some very old beliefs are that we learn best through suffering, and it is virtuous to be a martyr. Duality may be manmade; still, our experiences of pain and suffering can be very real. The more we focus on these "negatives", the more deeply ingrained in our realities they become. It's time to awaken from this nightmarish belief and let it go. Our souls first came to this planet to manifest into physical form--where duality is possible--so that they could experience deep contrast in order to evolve. Now, we are spiritually evolving beyond the need to suffer before we may become enlightened.

Peace. Peace is the next stage along our homo-luminous evolutionary track. Peace is not attained at the end, as many believe, hence the saying, "I'll have peace when I'm dead." No, peace is only the beginning, since it is not, as many also believe, a passive trait. It is dynamic, active, and vital, and it takes great willpower and self-mastery to maintain inner peace. Once inner peace is established, the mind is capable of expanding and the intellect becomes more focused on global progress and cooperation rather than on the petty dramas of our singular, brief lives.

Take a moment to imagine how much more productive you would be in your life if no drama existed, how much more satisfied and healthier you would be. Yes, this is what peace has to offer, and that's why inner peace is a necessary lesson in the core education of humanity. It's time for each of us to awaken to the realization of our grand importance and see just how we each impact the world.

The cosmic ocean is a collection of souls, just as our oceans are a collection of water droplets. It's time for us to purify ourselves and become the embodiment of peace. No longer can we wait for someone to come and save us from our suffering. Nor can we continue trying to fix other people's suffering while ignoring our own. It is time for us to step up and be responsible for the lives we have created and continue to create anew each morning.

My invitation to you: let the *Living Peace* tenets be your guiding compass into this new era that humanity is awakening to.

Acknowledgments

*I now take this moment to acknowledge and appreciate everyone I
have ever met in this lifetime. No matter how brief or long our
interactions, as humans, we are like vibrational keys to each other.
We energetically unlock doors of wisdom from the joy and contrast
we share, all of which promotes our growth.*

To my mom, Doreen Hutchinson, thank you for teaching me
the value of happiness early in life. Each morning you would
say to me, as I left for school, that the most important thing
was that I'd "be happy". I genuinely wish that every child
could have the same loving support and truly sage advice
while growing up — as it led me to be who I am today, a
peaceful man whose heart overflows with happiness. Both
you and Dad supported me unconditionally in my journey
towards inner peace and living a life of my own design, no
matter how off the beaten track and peculiar it may have
seemed to you at first. Thank you, and I love you both.

I especially want to take a moment to thank my dad, Ken
Hutchinson, since there is no story focused on him in the
book — even though he inherently embodies many of the
Living Peace Code's tenets. Never in my life have I ever heard
him utter a judgmental or prejudiced comment towards
anyone. It has taken me until my adulthood to realize just
how incredible (and rare) this is, and what a kind and giving
soul he has. Thank you, Dad, for not only supporting and
loving me, but for also being a fantastic role model of
unconditional acceptance and kindness towards people from
every walk of life.

Thank you, Andrew, for being my non-codependent
everything! Every day is a fun one as I share this lifetime with
you. We laugh together, and we learn together, with complete

and utter kindness, respect, warmth, and unconditional love. It truly is a wonderful and joyful experience being your husband! In the rewrite of this book, thank you for going above and beyond by reading every sentence aloud with me, and providing insightful feedback. Thank you for living these teachings with me and creating a life of literal, living peace with me. I love you.

Thank you to my grandparents, Harold and Jean, and my aunt, Kim, for equally supporting me. They each became pillars of loving support and generosity during the days of Earth Spirit Church, the first spiritual community I founded in Queen Creek, Arizona. I also want to thank the dozens of souls who were part of that community, whether they joined us briefly or continued on with us through its duration. Additionally, I extend my gratitude for all the memories made at Earth Spirit Center for Healing during my eight-year span with it.

Thank you, Emma Porter, for being a pillar of unconditional acceptance and support through the many phases of the center and church, and for now carrying the torch of peace in my stead in Arizona. Ella Wilson, thank you for seeing every part of my "box of crazy" and loving me anyway. Your friendship has truly been a divine blessing.

There are so many names I can list here since I never take any connection for granted. I am so honored to have met hundreds of people in Arizona, many of whom let me into their hearts and homes. Thank you for trusting in me and believing in the message of peace. I am grateful for my continued journey in Colorado now, with new communities and connections on the horizon. The world only knows where I may land next, yet wherever that may be, I take refuge in the loving heart of humanity.

To my editor — Shari Broyer — thank you for helping make this great book even better with your attention to detail and your mastery of the English language. Your service and your support, is always appreciated, and I recommend you 100%.

About the Author

Rev. Alaric Hutchinson — to his students, Sensei Alaric — has undertaken various spiritual leadership roles since 2010, when he opened his first business, Earth Spirit Center for Healing in Queen Creek, AZ. A year later, at just 22, he became a pastor and founded Earth Spirit Church. He led this spiritual community of fifty members for two years. After that, Alaric continued teaching classes each week and hosting community gatherings every Sunday. He also met with numerous clients to provide life coaching and spiritual guidance. Alaric sold his business, Earth Spirit Center, in April 2018 and moved to Bayfield, CO, with his husband, Andrew, in June 2018, to start their new life together. With nearly a decade of experience teaching peace and developing spiritual communities, Rev. Alaric is now a modern day Dunisha monk. Combining his past experiences of interfaith leadership with his present-day inner peace teachings through Zen mindfulness, Rev. Alaric aims to pastor a new community of people who are ready to embrace living peace.

Connect with Alaric

Alaric would love to meet and work with you! Visit his website for further information:

www.ZenCowboy.org

Visit with Alaric in Bayfield, Colorado at his new center for inner peace: The Zen Cowboy. Earth Spirit Center for Healing, in Queen Creek, AZ, is also still available to visit under its loving new ownership. In both states, you will find community with others who place an emphasis on Living Peace. Please feel free to reach out if you are seeking further connection after reading this book. Additionally, please contact Alaric if you desire to start your own community or group using the *Living Peace* teachings as an anchor. Training is available in person or long distance.

Want to be pen pals? Alaric loves receiving snail mail correspondence:

Alaric Hutchinson
P.O. Box 991
Bayfield, CO 81122

Want to make a donation? Please check The Zen Cowboy's website for community information and our 501c3 nonprofit status.

Also by the Author

- ➤ **5 Practices that Will Change Your Life**

- ➤ **Living Peace Philosophy**: An Introduction

Additional Books by Earth Spirit Publishing

- ➤ **Journey to Within**: One Woman's Glimpse into the Living Peace Code
  by Emma Porter

All books are available in print on Amazon. Be sure to occasionally check our website: **www.ZenCowboy.org** for added audio and e-book options.

Please remember to write a review on our Amazon pages.

Thank you!

Printed in Great Britain
by Amazon